HOW TO
HIRE,
TRAIN
& keep
THE BEST
EMPLOYEES
for Your Small Business

Dianna Podmoroff, BA, MBA, CHRP

How to Hire, Train and Keep the Best Employees for Your Small Business—With Companion CD-ROM

Atlantic Publishing Group, Inc. Copyright © 2005
1210 SW 23rd Place
Ocala, Florida 34474
800-541-1336
352-622-5836–Fax
www.atlantic-pub.com–Web site
sales@atlantic-pub.com–E-mail

SAN Number :268-1250

International Standard Book Number: 0-910627-37-1

Library of Congress Cataloging-in-Publication Data

Podmoroff, Dianna.
  How to hire, train & keep the best employees for your small business :
with companion CD-Rom / Dianna Podmoroff.
        p. cm.
  Includes bibliographical references and index.
  ISBN 0-910627-37-1 (alk. paper)
  1. Small business--Personnel management. 2. Employees--Recruiting. 3.
Employees--Training of. I. Title: How to hire, train and keep the best
employees for your small business. II. Title.

  HF5549.P574 2004
  658.3--dc22
                        2004015355

Print in the United States

Book cover, layout and design by Meg Buchner of Megadesign
www.mega-designs.com • e-mail: megadesn@mchsi.com

TABLE OF CONTENTS

Chapter 1
SUCCESSFUL RECRUITMENT STRATEGIES

Chapter 2
INTERVIEWING AND HIRING THE RIGHT WAY

Chapter 3
EFFECTIVE COMMUNICATION

Chapter 4
TRAINING

Chapter 5
MOTIVATION

Chapter 6
LEADERSHIP AND TEAM-BUILDING

Chapter 7
EMPLOYEE RETENTION ESSENTIALS

We recently lost our beloved pet "Bear," who was not only our best and dearest friend but also the "Vice President of Sunshine" here at Atlantic Publishing. He did not receive a salary but worked tirelessly 24 hours a day to please his parents. Bear was a rescue dog that turned around and showered myself, my wife Sherri, his grandparents Jean, Bob and Nancy and every person and animal he met (maybe not rabbits) with friendship and love. He made a lot of people smile every day.

We wanted you to know that a portion of the profits of this book will be donated to The Humane Society of the United States.

–Douglas & Sherri Brown

THE HUMANE SOCIETY
OF THE UNITED STATES ©

The human-animal bond is as old as human history. We cherish our animal companions for their unconditional affection and acceptance. We feel a thrill when we glimpse wild creatures in their natural habitat or in our own backyard.

Unfortunately, the human-animal bond has at times been weakened. Humans have exploited some animal species to the point of extinction.

The Humane Society of the United States makes a difference in the lives of animals here at home and worldwide. The HSUS is dedicated to creating a world where our relationship with animals is guided by compassion. We seek a truly humane society in which animals are respected for their intrinsic value, and where the human-animal bond is strong.

Want to help animals? We have plenty of suggestions. Adopt a pet from a local shelter, join The Humane Society and be a part of our work to help companion animals and wildlife. You will be funding our educational, legislative, investigative and outreach projects in the U.S. and across the globe.

Or perhaps you'd like to make a memorial donation in honor of a pet, friend or relative? You can through our Kindred Spirits program. And if you'd like to contribute in a more structured way, our Planned Giving Office has suggestions about estate planning, annuities, and even gifts of stock that avoid capital gains taxes.

Maybe you have land that you would like to preserve as a lasting habitat for wildlife. Our Wildlife Land Trust can help you. Perhaps the land you want to share is a backyard—that's enough. Our Urban Wildlife Sanctuary Program will show you how to create a habitat for your wild neighbors.

So you see, it's easy to help animals. And The HSUS is here to help.

The Humane Society of the United States
2100 L Street NW
Washington, DC 20037
202-452-1100
www.hsus.org

INTRODUCTION

Getting the right people in the right job and then getting them to stay are the key elements in effective business organizations. It sounds quite straightforward, and many mangers and business owners simply put an ad in the local paper, wait for the applications to arrive, do some requisite interviewing, and then hire the people they liked the best. Boom, done—now they've got people in place doing the jobs that need to be done and the business is ready to roll! Then all hell starts breaking loose; there are attendance problems, attitude problems and personality conflicts: the business is suffering, the employees are suffering, and management is barely able to keep the ship afloat. What went wrong?

The short answer is they hired the wrong people; they failed to make human resource management a priority and assumed that bodies in positions would run the company regardless of any careful consideration given to getting the right bodies in the right places. The good news is that careful planning and strategic management of the recruitment, hiring and retention processes will greatly improve your business's success; the bad news is that HR management is not an exact science because people are unpredictable. Fortunately, there are many strategies, techniques and practices that have been proven to improve all aspects of people management; after all, your people are your business, and your human resources are the most important resource your business has; it makes sense to manage them just as diligently as you manage your financial, technological and other business resources.

These are the skills you'll learn in *How to Hire, Train & Keep the Best Employees for Your Small Business*. This book covers all the essential elements of employee management in an easy-to understand and practical manner. Topics include:

- Successful Recruitment Strategies — how to find good, potential employees.

- Hiring and Interviewing — asking the right questions, the right way.

- Effective Communication — giving and receiving information effectively.

- Training — improving employee performance.

- Motivation — creating job satisfaction.

- Leadership and Team-Building — influencing employees to work effectively.

There are lots of examples, case studies, exercises and activities that will reinforce the ideas presented and give you useful tools to implement in and customize to your own organization. Great companies start with great people, and by reading this book, you are well on your way.
Enjoy!

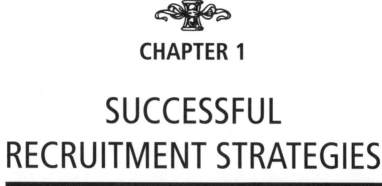

CHAPTER 1

SUCCESSFUL RECRUITMENT STRATEGIES

How to Find Good, Potential Employees

*"The best thing we can do for
our competitors is hire poorly."*

—Recruiting Director, Microsoft

Good selection of employees results in many advantages for the manger and the organization, and invariably results in decreased costs for the business. The top five reasons are:

Increased Output

The most productive employee is usually twice as productive as the least productive employee. Certainly the mangers and the organization benefit when more highly productive employees are hired.

Reduced Training Time

As training becomes more complicated and expensive, the speed that an individual can learn a new job becomes more important. Some individuals catch on to new tasks or responsibilities quickly and become much faster than others. The organization and the individuals benefit when new employees reach minimum productivity requirements in the shortest amount of time.

Better Use of Managers' Training and Coaching Time

The manager often spends a great deal of time bringing one poor employee up to the minimum performance level. However, when all members of the work group meet minimum performance levels, the manger can spend the same time bringing several employees up to higher levels of productivity. Most mangers would choose the latter use of time. Certainly the organization benefits from having more skillful employees, but the employees themselves also benefit. Individuals who work at levels that are well above the minimum requirement have a greater sense of achievement and self-worth, and are usually better rewarded.

Decreased Turnover

Many organizations do not realize how much it actually costs them to hire and train a new employee. Various expenses must be considered, including the personnel specialist's time, advertising, operating without an individual in the position (overtime for other employees, loss of sales, poor customer service, etc.), training, and lower productivity during the training period.

Organizations and technology continue to become more complicated, so more training is required to bring new employees up to acceptable productivity levels. For example, a new insurance salesperson costs a company about $15,000 before becoming even slightly productive, and $65,000 before the salesperson starts making money for the company. An operator of a nuclear plant receives more than $1,000,000 in training before being allowed to work in the plant.

Increased Time to Manage

In addition to training, a manager must plan, organize and control the various elements of his or her responsibility. This becomes much harder when he or she must spend time "fighting fires" caused by poor employees. Managers usually spend 60 percent of their time dealing with matters that concern 5–10 percent of their workforce: some employees are late or absent, again and again; others are forever having problems with fellow employees. Problems are always going to crop up, but most managers have probably thought about how much more they could accomplish if they had fewer poor employees.

THE RECRUITMENT PROCESS

Prepare a Job Description

In today's competitive labor environment, it is important that the hiring process be approached in an organized manner. First, you need to define the qualifications of the individual being sought by preparing a formal job description. The purpose of the description is threefold:

1. Specify what type of person and skills are needed for the job.

2. Outline to potential hires what the position will involve.

3. Describe the scope of the position and how it contributes to the company.

While many businesses tend to put off developing formal job descriptions, it is a necessary evil of sorts that will pay off immeasurably in the recruitment and hiring process. Remember, good hiring practices mean hiring the right person the first time. The best (and only!) way to know who the right person is comes from a clear analysis of the position and a full understanding of what the expectations of the position are. (See the end of this chapter for job description template form.)

Example

Do-It-Yourself Plumbing needs a receptionist. They place an ad in their local paper:

> ## RECEPTIONIST NEEDED
> Mon–Fri 9:00 a.m. to 5:00 p.m.
> Must have previous reception
> experience, be organized, and
> work well independently.
> Send applications to 677 Little John
> Road, Plymouth, MA 02360.

The ad was quite successful in terms of the quantity of responses, so Larry and Bob were able to short-list only those applicants with over 5 years of experience as a receptionist. They went into the interviews very confident that their perfect employee was waiting to meet them. Nothing was further from the truth when in the interviews they asked the candidates about their abilities in such activities as tracking accounts payable and receivable invoices, issuing work orders and preparing company correspondence. All of the short-listed applicants had experience in a few of the duties mentioned, but none of them could do it all. Do-It-Yourself Plumbing was a new company that needed help answering the phones, but in order to justify a full-time position, the receptionist would have to do a variety of general office administration duties as well, and neither Bob nor Larry had much spare time to train so the person chosen had to be very competent in all the elements before starting the position.

This is the exact type of situation where preparing a job description would have helped Bob and Larry to fully understand their position requirements and then advertise accordingly. It does not mean spending inordinate amounts of time writing verbose work statements; it simply means getting a solid picture of the ideal candidate in your mind before actively recruiting. The form of the job description is variable, but the elements that need to be included are:

- **Corporate overview** (synthesis of the company's business, market, history, facilities and goals).

- **Position title** and to whom to report.

- **Description of the responsibilities** and authorities of the position.

- **Experience required**: work background, technical knowledge, qualifications needed.

- **Personal characteristics**: education, personality traits,

interpersonal skills.
- **Compensation**: wage or salary, other payment plans, benefit package.

Unfortunately, the adage, "I'll know it when I see it" does not apply to the selection process, and none of us have the time, energy or patience to go through unnecessary interviews with candidates who are less than minimally capable of the job.

Decide on a Recruiting Method

There are many different avenues available to you to reach prospective candidates, and it is very important to consider which method will reach the greatest number of qualified applicants in the most cost-effective way. Some of the most common methods include:

- Print advertising: newspapers, trade magazines, professional associations

- Internet: job boards, company Web site

- Radio

- Job fairs

- Recruitment firms: executive search, recruitment agency, temp services

- Referrals: employees, customers

- College recruiting

Each method has its own costs and benefits associated with it, and it is your responsibility to determine which method is best for the position you are currently recruiting. While Internet recruiting can be the cheapest way to advertise, it is also the method that tends to get the most unqualified responses, but if you're looking for a technical position, it almost behooves you to use a job board or other technologically savvy technique. One human resource director recently said, "If it's an information technology position, I'm going to go online; I'm going to get 1,000 résumés, but if it's technology-based, that's where you need to go." Very specialized or high-level positions are often best filled using the services of a professional search firm that has the time and contacts needed to "head-hunt" the perfect candidate for you.

In 2001, the Society for Human Resource Management (SHRM) conducted a survey of top job search tactics, and here's what they found:

Tactic Used	% of Job Seekers Who Use	% of Job Seekers Find Effective
Internet job postings	96%	48%
Personal contact/networking	95%	78%
Ads in newspapers	95%	30%
Employee referrals/ employee referral program	92%	65%
Online or Web site job applications	90%	>10%
Headhunters	>10%	45%

The key factor for you to consider is you what you intend to accomplish and how to do it most efficiently. Because cost is a big factor in deciding which method to use, it is important to use each medium most effectively. The following is a discussion of the most cost-effective recruiting methods and some tips and considerations that can be used to maximize your recruiting returns.

PRINT ADVERTISING

The classifieds section of a newspaper has been the traditional first step for companies looking to fill vacant positions; however, it is not as simple as it appears. The right ad in the right newspaper can make your résumé basket overflow with qualified candidates. The wrong ad, or the wrong newspaper, can leave you with one or two applicants who may not be quite what you are looking for. The following are some guidelines to follow for recruitment advertising.

Where to Advertise

Putting your ad in the right newspaper is a critical first step for placing employment ads, and targeting your ad within the right newspaper is of the utmost importance. Typically, a large urban center will have four or five major daily newspapers with large circulations from which to choose. It is very important to determine each paper's target demographic market, and then place your ad accordingly. Senior executives and other professionals will tend to favor papers with in-depth business and international sections; tradespeople usually lean more toward papers that provide concise summaries of the top local and national news; and clerical personnel often read the

Determine the newspaper's target demographic market, and then place your ad accordingly.

smaller and more localized community and specialized papers. If you're recruiting individuals in specialized fields, trade publications often reach the best venue. Because there are so many alternatives available, it is necessary to do your homework and find out which paper's readership is the best fit for the position you are recruiting.

Writing the Ad

In today's tight labor market, getting job candidates to respond to recruitment advertising can be tough, and to be effective, recruitment messages need to sell the opportunity, using a marketing approach as follows.

Balance the Message

Your ad needs to appeal to the candidates you want and, at the same time, screen out the candidates you don't want. This is a tenuous balance that requires careful consideration of the

amount and extent of detail you provide in your ad. If you
are advertising for a routine position, the use of qualifiers
will reduce the response rate by discouraging some job
candidates. Consider the following qualifiers:

- If you have . . .

- Some . . . preferred

- Must have . . .

- No beginners, please.

- Minimum of . . .

- . . . mandatory

- . . . helpful

- Background checks will be conducted.

Sell the Position

The question that all ads, help-wanted or otherwise, need
to address is the "What's in it for me?" factor. This is
where your careful analysis of the job description and your
company come into play — you need to know the most
attractive things you offer potential employees in exchange
for their talent. Such benefits include health insurance, paid
vacation, retirement plans, etc. Benefits are the important
selling tools for small firms, and many people don't think
small businesses offer them, so for that reason it's important

to mention as many as possible. Your classified ad needs to stand out from all the other ads on the page; you must "sell" the candidate on your company so they contact you instead of the other companies whose ads surround yours.

Emphasize Critical Elements

It is important to let potential applicants know the primary functions of the job. Critical elements might include certain computer skills, communication skills, hours worked, travel involved, sales skills, etc. By adding these essential qualifications, you weed out many non-qualified candidates. It is also important to include some information about the company in the ad. A particular position may appeal to many people, but the corporate culture may not be a good fit for the person; some employers value creative thinking, others emphasize independence, and others stress strict adherence to policy and procedures. These subtle differences in the job make for huge differences in terms of applicant suitability, and it is important that an employee's personality, skills and experience fit the job.

Use Headlines

The job title is the most common ad headline and the least interesting. A recruitment ad headline should be designed to grab the readers' attention; remember, you are often competing with many other recruitment messages, and your message must stand out to be effective. The ad on the next page for an optical center is a good example.

Some headline examples include:

- Are you customer-service focused?

- We're working overtime to get you here part-time!

- Are YOU our next . . .

- You think we're a great place to shop . . . now think about us as a great place to work!

The messages are simple and direct, and they use the most coveted word in advertising: "You." Using the word "you" personalizes the message and gets the reader thinking about what's in it for them. Other words with marketing or recruitment appeal are "new," "opportunity," "exciting" and "management."

Make the Message Interesting

You likely have a lot of information to convey to job seekers, but you need to keep the ad short enough so that it doesn't read like a shopping list and interesting enough to keep the readers' attention. Most employment ads are simply abbreviated job descriptions listing task after task, and boring even the most dedicated job seeker. To encourage readability, make the tone of your ad conversational, and talk directly to the reader using pronouns like "you" and "we."

Impersonal	Conversational
"The candidate will demonstrate exceptional interpersonal skills."	*"You will relate to us with a great degree of finesse."*

This change makes it sound like you are talking to the applicant directly and the reader can see themselves as the successful candidate.

- **Use action-oriented verbs to sell your position.** Don't simply state the facts, "This is a great opportunity" but create excitement by saying, "Seize this opportunity." Action verbs motivate people to act, and after they read the ad, they will be more likely to apply for the position.

- **Talk to the audience in their language.** The same copy that would attract a registered nurse would never catch the interest of an I.T. professional. In either case, they are looking for a company that understands them and can speak their language.

- **Use a logical flow to help the reader better understand your message.** Start with a captivating headline to hook the reader, and then hold their interest by giving some of the highlights of the job description. Now that the reader is interested, you can introduce the drier job requirements information at the end of the ad. Make sure to be concise and get the salient points across quickly before you lose the reader to the next ad.

AGRICULTURAL DIESEL MECHANIC

Would you like to work in New Zealand? We are looking for a qualified Diesel Mechanic to work on a variety of tractors and other farm equipment. Have a look at our Web site, www.norwood.co.nz. Taranaki is a great place to live and work—have a look at http://www. destination-nz.co.nz/new-plymouth/. If you are interested, drop me a line: Rhona McLean, 146 Gill Street, New Plymouth, New Zealand, 0000 Tel: +64067575582, or e-mail 888@tylco.nz.

This simple ad has it all: it attracts diesel mechanics that are specific to agricultural equipment (a qualifier) and it has an enticing byline, "Would you like to work in New Zealand?" Because anyone qualified as an agricultural diesel mechanic will likely have the same requisite skills, this ad focuses on getting the candidate to check out the company Web site and find information on the location. Interested candidates will likely go to both Web sites and then self-select so that only qualified and truly interested applications will be received.

Of course, once the content is presented correctly, an ad can also be improved graphically. The ad below has the same information, but utilizes distinguishing techniques and graphics to get noticed.

AGRICULTURAL DIESEL MECHANIC WANTED

Would you like to work in New Zealand?
We are looking for a qualified Diesel Mechanic to work on a variety of tractors and other farm equipment. Visit our Web site, www.norwood.co.nz. Taranaki is a great place to live and work—have a look at http://www.destination-nz.co.nz/new-plymouth/.

If you are interested, drop me a line:
Rhona McLean, 146 Gill Street, New Plymouth, New Zealand, 0000
Tel: +64067575582, or e-mail 888@tylco.nz

Ad Design
Here again, you are trying to distinguish yourself from your competitors. Some ideas for an interesting ad design include:

Use Graphics
Use photos and illustrations to break outside the normal border of the rectangular ad. This will necessitate some extra distance from neighboring ads and will draw the reader's eye. It is also a creative and interesting use of space that will appeal to many people. Remember that graphics need a fair amount of white space to have impact, and they need to be relevant to your text so don't use them just for the sake of using them.

Change the Shape

Enclose your ad in a circle or a triangle rather than the usual and expected rectangle. Work with the publisher to set yourself apart by using billboard- (extreme horizontal) or skyscraper- (extreme vertical) style ads.

Wouldn't You Like to Stop and Smell the Roses?

If you enjoy posies and plants and are seeking a relaxed, casual work environment, consider The Blooming Basket. We are seeking someone to assist with floral arrangements and deliveries. Flexible hours. Call 453-555-2983 or inquire in person at:

The Blooming Basket
424 West Garden Street
Roselyn, NY 54670

Use Color and Contrast

Color adds impact, and studies have shown that full-color ads receive 40 percent greater readership than other ads in the same publication. If cost is an issue, the alternative is to use contrast: reversed print, white letters on a black background or no screens or tints are methods that create a really high-contrast look that will stand out from the crowd.

Use White Space

Ads should include plenty of white space because it increases readability. The problem is that it is expensive, but it is one of the most effective design tricks to make your message stand out. Using bullets creates more white space: use them to break up copy and highlight key points; this will help the reader scan the ad and increase the likelihood of response.

Be Concise

The best messages are short, simple and concise. Most of the competition will use lengthy job description and company narratives so your "simple" ad will stand out. Include the most relevant information and keep the interest level high.

Make It Easy to Apply

This is more important than you might think as often the decision to send a résumé or application depends upon the convenience of making the contact. Wherever possible, use phone calls, faxes, e-mail and "snail mail" as options. Remember, this easy accessibility is open to everyone so you want to have as many qualifiers as necessary in your ad to discourage unqualified applications.

Recruitment ads can represent up to 50 percent of the total selection process cost in time and expenses. Optimizing the size of the ad and communicating the right information will save you money. Add to that the costs associated with sifting through stacks of résumés from unsuitable candidates and you have some very compelling reasons to think strategically about recruitment ads, and not just follow the carbon-copy variety we see in papers today.

Just as the ads themselves are changing, getting flashier and more directed to sell an applicant on the job, the places where jobs are advertised are also changing. Recruitment ads are finding their way into the main section of the newspaper, where they can catch the eye of an unsuspecting job seeker (a worker who otherwise is not scouring help-wanted ads on a daily basis, but is very much worth recruiting efforts). Billboard ads are also a trend (an expensive one, though!), as are advertising on a corporate Web site or on the radio.

RADIO ADVERTISING

Traditional advertising methods require the job seeker to find the message; this works reasonably well because most people looking for jobs are doing so actively. But the percentage of active job seekers in the workplace is actually quite low, so a well-rounded recruitment campaign targets the passive job seeker as well. These people might currently work at your competitor's workplace, and you may be able to entice them to work for you if they know you're looking. Radio does this because it is intrusive: the message finds the listener. And it is very easy to find out who the listener

A radio campaign reaches the passive job seeker—
perhaps even at at your competitor's workplace.

will be because radio stations gather extensive demographic information on their audience so they can sell advertising effectively.

With radio advertising, your ad will not likely be surrounded with other competing job spots so you get exclusive access to your market, but because radio is targeting passive listeners, you will need a number of short spots to catch the audience's attention. This may seem unnecessary compared to running one ad in the paper, but radio reaches 77 percent of persons 12 and over on a daily basis, making it a very powerful medium. And, the radio spots are more likely to reach your current employees as well; this indicates to them that they are working at a cool and progressive company, and that you are doing everything you can to get more or better employees to make the workplace strong. Radio is a very effective source for recruitment advertising, but it is a frequency medium so you must buy more than a few spots. Depending on your target applicant, the current job market and the number of qualified people in the industry you are recruiting, radio may be a very cost-effective alternative to the more traditional forms of advertising.

INTERNET POSTING

Internet recruiting is more than just posting your newspaper ad online. Unlike print advertising, with Internet job postings, you do not pay by the line or the column inch, so you can provide as much additional information as you need to answer most (if not all) of a candidate's initial questions. When job boards first started popping up in the early 1990s, not many employers or job seekers took notice; now, a

Over 95 percent of job seekers use the Internet to source jobs, and over 40 percent say the Internet is their preferred method.

decade later, over 95 percent of job seekers use the Internet to source jobs, and over 40 percent say the Internet is their preferred method. The popularity of the Internet is a double-edged sword; with some recruiters delighted by the continuous flow of résumés they receive, and others struggling to stay afloat on top of the river of applications, many unqualified, that come in for every position posted.

The most compelling reason to use Internet advertising is the cost, and if you employ the same qualifying techniques talked about with print ads, you are likely to get a high number of top-quality applications. The average price for an online job posting is $300 compared to $500 in a major newspaper (2003), and the online posting is usually available for 30–60 days versus a one-day run in the Career section of the paper. There are smaller, niche-market job boards that can be accessed for as little as $24 per month. Despite the availability of these cheaper alternatives, the large boards like Monster, Hot Jobs, and Headhunters remain the best choice for the majority of employers because job seekers recognize these brand names and are more likely to visit the site. Small- to medium-sized businesses are especially keen on using professional sites because they don't typically have the time or resources available to offer Internet recruiting on their own corporate site. Also, if relocation costs are going to be an issue, then using a local service is the only feasible alternative. The critique of job boards centers around the fact that they are cold and impersonal compared to the highly interpersonal process of hiring someone. It is a very isolated and non-interactive way to look for and post a job.

Small businesses are being offered incentives to use the large boards once considered the domain of large corporations. Cost effectiveness is the key and the industry realizes that the small business does not have a dedicated HR professional, let alone a recruiter, and so the president is left to find the employees and then sweep up after them. If you do decide to use the Internet to post your jobs, you want to get the most for your money, so to follow are some guidelines to follow.

Elements of an Internet Job Posting
Job Title
This is the first thing a prospective applicant will see, and it is the search term most often used. What will differentiate your sales or programmer ad from all the rest? Use a creative job title like "Sassy & Super Salesperson" or "Particular Programmer for Particularly High Wages Needed."

Company Information

This section is very important, and it is the big advantage to posting online. You can give the applicant all the information they need to self-select themselves for the job and address the most common concerns that job seekers have. You should include the following information:

- Brief description of the organization.

- Products and/or services your company provides.

- Define your corporate culture.

- What type of training and career path they can expect.

- Why your company is a good place to work.

- Work environment (example: casual, formal, team-focused, telecommuting, flex hours, etc.).

All of this information helps "sell" your company to candidates.

Job Description

Candidates want to know the expectations of the position; although you have more room on the Internet to list all the activities, try to keep it more interesting than a bulleted list of duties all starting with the words "responsible for." Besides some key duties, include their relevance to the company as a whole and some insight into the work environment:

- Detailed overview of the responsibilities the position entails.

- General scope of the work.

- Will they be part of a team, managing a team, or working independently?

- Reason for position opening (growth, expansion, new opening, etc.).

- Role the position and department has within the organization.

When job seekers are finished reading this section, they will have a mental picture of the type of work they will be doing.

Required Qualifications

List your strict requirements (the skills that are absolutely essential) and then include information on the bonus qualifications and experience for which you are looking. Include the following:

- Desired or minimum number of years of specific experience.

- Work history.

- Education or certifications needed.

- Soft skills (example: time management, organization skills, leadership, communications skills, willingness to travel, etc.).

Application Process

Let the candidates know how to apply, remembering that the more options you give, the easier it will be for them to send in their résumé and the more response you are likely to get.

- E-mail — the fastest and easiest way to receive résumés.

- Fax number.

- Phone number.

- Mailing address.

- Web site — offer link to the home page or the Employment section within your Web site.

Keywords

In order for job seekers to find your ad amongst the hundreds or even thousands of ads on the site, you must include any and all of the keywords that a qualified applicant would think to search. The more keywords you use in the posting, the more "hits" you'll get.

Example:

Keywords for posting for a Controller position:

- Accounting
- Accountant
- CPA

- CMA
- CFO
- Finance
- Accounting Director
- Accounting Manger
- Director of Finance
- Accounting Manager

These Internet posting basics and ads that follow the rules of newspaper advertising (targeted, descriptive and attention-grabbing) will help you achieve a successful recruiting strategy on the Internet and should get you more response than by newspaper alone.

REFERRAL PROGRAMS

Word-of-mouth, or employee referral, can be the most effective means of attracting new, qualified recruits, and it is usually the most cost efficient because candidates who learn about a company through an existing employee tend to be a better fit and stay with the company longer. This makes sense because the candidate is usually well acquainted with the current employee and is very familiar with the company, this should alleviate most of the questions about "fit" since the person understands and is interested in the corporate culture. The referring employee can also vouch for the candidate's character, which is one of the hardest elements to judge in an interview. And, bottom line, people enjoy working with people they like and they certainly wouldn't refer someone they felt they, or their coworkers, couldn't get along with.

There is an onus on the referring employee to send only the

Referrals are usually a good fit since they are already familiar with the company and employees.

most qualified people to the hiring manager's door because if the recruit does poorly, that will reflect negatively on his or her judgment. The higher quality of the recruit and the likelihood of a good fit, shortens the hiring cycle, thus decreasing costs; both directly related to the new hire as well as opportunity costs associated with turnover.

Elements of a Referral Program
Referral Incentive
It is a common practice for companies to increase the incentive for their employees to refer new recruits by paying them for each person who joins the firm and stays beyond a certain term, say three or six months. In order to avoid a rash amount of referrals, the incentive should also be applied to long-term successful applicants; you certainly don't want a revolving door of poorly referred employees. Non-monetary incentives are also popular: gift certificates, golf day with the

boss, extended weekend or company tickets to a sporting event.

Communication

All employees must have access to the program, know that it exists and know how to use it. Companies must take advantage of the company newsletter, Intranet, e-mail system, bulletin boards and management meetings to spread

Take advantage of your company's Intranet or bulletin board.

the word about the program. Some companies choose to talk directly with employees they consider exemplar, asking them for their personal referrals. The notion of being singled out is very motivating to not only refer candidates but to continue performing at a high level.

Dos and Don'ts

Do not hype a referral program if your industry or company is in a slowdown or hiring freeze. It is insulting and condescending to offer a referral carrot with no hope of ever cashing in. In industries with chronic shortages, like health care and teaching, referral programs are absolutely necessary to bolster the number of applicants. If your company is suffering with low morale or other negative work environment influences, it is important to address the internal issues before adding any new staff to the company, referred or not. Dissatisfied employees will not tend to refer high-quality employees and, more than likely, the referred employees will simply be taking the place of all your current employees as they exit.

Get Creative

Finding great people is the number-one priority for many organizations, and it will remain that way for some time to come. Recruitment is often frustrating, but a little excitement and creativity can go a long way to bring in new talent.

See the case study for Enterprise Rent-A-Car on the following page. Beyond simply recruiting and securing new employees, Enterprise used creativity to draw the best out of people—a process that was not only professionally satisfying, but a great deal of fun.

Other types of creative recruiting activities include internship programs, college career fairs, vocational schools, job fairs, trade shows, Internet banners, retirees' referrals and alumni initiatives.

Case Study—Enterprise Rent-A-Car	
Problem: In 2000, Enterprise Rent-A-Car had to fill 6,000 positions across North America	**Solution:** Hold a "Promote Yourself" career contest

Details: Job applicants were invited to demonstrate their creativity by applying for a job at Enterprise in a non-traditional fashion; they were invited to submit their most creative résumé, be it a Web page, CD-ROM, painting or poetry. The only rule was that their entry had to fit through the door.

There were prizes for the top six entries and, of course, the opportunity to work in a management training position at Enterprise. The contest was very successful and Enterprise received many creative entries as well as traditional job applications. The creativity was endless and applications covered the spectrum from original jingles, poems and essays, to paintings on canvas, interactive Web sites and three-dimensional models. Canadian Erin Marsden, ranked first out of six North American winners with her Web site résumé. Other winning entries included home videos, a paper pizza (which listed the applicant's qualifications under each slice), a game board, CD-ROM, and a man's shoe bearing the caption, "Now that I've got my foot in the door..."

TIPS TO MAXIMIZE YOUR RECRUITMENT DOLLAR

Use Free Web Sites to Post Openings

There are literally thousands of sites on the Internet created to accept postings of your job openings. Although the prices are rising rapidly, it is amazing what you can find out there that is free of charge. An excellent job site that is free of charge is America's Job Bank. After a quick registration and verification of your company data, you get free job postings and access to a searchable database of over 600,000 résumés. Also worth checking into are trade association sites of which you or one of your employees is a member; often they give free job postings to affiliated members.

Also, local colleges and universities typically have a Web site

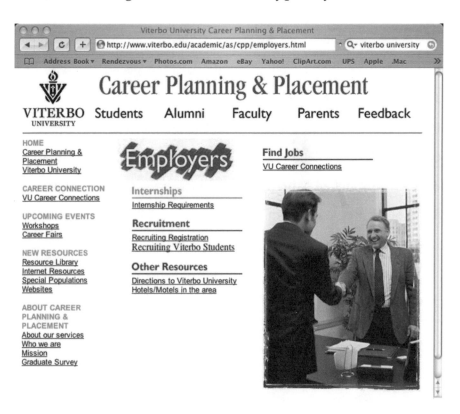

with career planning and job openings. You can usually have your job listed there free of charge and not only have access to recent graduates, but alumni as well.

Combine Ads When Possible

Instead of posting three separate positions and reiterating the company information each time, try to combine the ads. Your ad will be larger and thus attract more attention, and it should be cheaper than three smaller ads.

Direct applicants to your corporate site for job details and other information. It isn't necessary to give prospects a complete rundown on every little detail about the job, the requirements, etc. Make your print ad shorter: you'll save money, the brevity will set it apart from the others, you'll likely get a higher response rate, and the prospect will visit your Web site if they want more information.

Source Your Prior Applicants for Current Job Openings

Before spending money on additional advertising, review the applications you received from prior postings. This may mean going through stacks of old résumés so be forward-thinking the next time you receive a bunch of résumés and categorize them with future positions in mind. There are also many affordable applicant-tracking systems that will keep the names and contact information of all your in-house résumés just a click away. If you are in an industry with typically high turnover or you expect to hire frequently, investing in one of these systems may be very cost effective in the medium- to long-term.

Use the Lowest-Cost-per-Hire Techniques

It sounds obvious but do you know which methods
are consistently the cheapest? In 2002, the Employment
Management Association (EMA) found the average cost-per-
hire for the main recruitment sources was:

Source	Cost per Hire
Print Advertising	$1,886
Job Fairs	$1,800
Contingency Search	$18,374
Executive Search	$61,330
Employee Referral	$640
Internet	$888
College Recruiting	$5,020

It makes sense to use referral programs and the Internet to
recruit new employees and save the professional services for
those positions where qualified talent is scarce or the cost of
making a hiring mistake is huge.

Continuously Improve

Some recruitment methods have been very successful for you
in the past and some you think have been utter disasters. To
truly understand which methods have been cost effective
though, you have to track the cost-per-hire. With a little ad-
tracking you may be surprised to learn which campaigns were
really the most successful, and then you can build on those
results for the next time.

When looking to recruit top-quality people, it is important to treat the process just as seriously as you would any new venture or strategy; innovation, creativity and solid planning are essential and will help to ensure you get the best possible people applying for your jobs.

To recruit top-quality people, treat the process just as seriously as you would any new venture.

Job Description Template

Job Title: _____   Company Job Code: _____

FLSA Status: _____   Division/Department: _____

EEO Code: _____   Reports to: _____

Salary Grade/Band: _____   Last Revision Date: _____

SUMMARY

This section provides an overall summary of the job.

ADDITIONAL RESPONSIBILITIES

This section provides additional functions of the job. The responsibilities are usually desired but not required. These duties are not "essential functions"; therefore, even if an applicant cannot perform these duties, the applicants will still be considered for the position.

PRIMARY RESPONSIBILITIES

This section provides the primary functions of the job. The responsibilities are usually in order of importance and/or time spent. This list may also be used to define "essential functions" for the purposes of the Americans with Disabilities Act. Therefore, duties listed here should be considered "essential". If an applicant cannot perform most if not all of the essential functions, the applicant will not be considered for the position.

KNOWLEDGE AND SKILL REQUIREMENTS

This section provides specific knowledge and skill requirements such as sales techniques, facilitation skills, generally accepted accounting principles, and physical requirements. The number of years of experience and/or education requirements are also listed here.

WORKING CONDITIONS

This section contains information on working conditions out of the ordinary such as extensive travel, high noise levels, and frequent lifting of over X pounds.

ACKNOWLEDGMENT

This section provides dated signature lines for the manager/supervisor and employee. This provides a record that the employee was shown and understands the job responsibilities.

Name (print)_____ Signature_____ Date:_____

CHAPTER 2

INTERVIEWING
AND HIRING THE RIGHT WAY

Asking the Right Questions, the Right Way

*"Employers who use informal
interviews and résumés to make
hiring decisions are taking a gamble."*

—*John H. Eggers, Professor, Richard Ivey School of Business*

Research from the Richard Ivey School of Business in London, Ontario, shows that nearly one-quarter of the people hired by the traditional methods of interviewing and reviewing résumés will fail. These tried-but-not-true methods do not predict or identify high-performance employees, so the right people are not always getting hired for the job. Also on the rise from time-strapped managers is the practice of leaving hiring decisions to instinct. This study revealed that most hiring decisions are still based on the following three approaches:

- **Warm body** — in a panic, employers hire anyone who looks good at the time.

- **Rituals** — traditional methods will suffice, regardless of rational evidence that suggests there are better approaches.

- **Gut feeling** — managers use their intuition to make hiring decisions.

The selection process demands a rigorous and strategically analyzed system to function effectively and consistently deliver top-performing employees. The following are some guidelines to follow when developing your own selection process.

Good selection begins with good recruitment, and you need to be honest with candidates from the start including the good and bad aspects of the job. Working conditions and compensation need to be clearly established so that potential candidates have the opportunity to decide for themselves if they are a fit for your company. If they don't feel they "fit," then you are wasting your time interviewing them.

An effective selection method focuses on what the job really is, gets relevant information from a candidate, and provides a framework for making rational and fair decisions in the hiring process. To supplement the interviewing process, many companies are using ability or aptitude testing; these methods, when the information is combined with structured interviews, add considerable predictive power to the selection battery and are one of the best ways employers have to predict the future performance of a candidate.

Basically, hiring is a "pay now or pay later" proposition, and if you are reluctant to spend time and money on the selection process, you will undoubtedly pay in terms of employee turnover, productivity, morale, and the like.

SCREENING APPLICATIONS

If you've done your homework and created an effective recruiting campaign, then you should have some good-quality résumés and applications to weed through to make a short-list. Résumés come in a variety of formats and styles, so it is important to look at them objectively and not judge an applicant on the aesthetics of the résumé itself. Of course, if the position you are hiring is expected to have superior communication skills, then the résumé and cover letter are good indicators of the applicant's skill level; you would expect a well-worded and grammatically sound résumé for a management or administrative position, whereas a senior scientist or machine operator may be forgiven for straightforward wording and the occasional dangling participle.

What's important on the résumé is how well the applicant's skills and experience relate to your job opening. The best and most defensible way to approach the screening process is with a screening worksheet. The worksheet sets out specific skills, knowledge and experience that are important to the job at hand and gets the screener to rate the applicant accordingly.

The screening characteristics will change with every position and may include very specific qualifications like C++ programmer, MBA, CGA, etc. Some worksheets apply weights to the various characteristics listed and then get a weighted total for comparison purposes. Regardless of the specific system you use, it is important to structure the process and keep the selection process as unbiased and nondiscriminatory as possible. This helps you short-list the best applicants for the job and it satisfies any legal requirements your state has for equal opportunity employment.

An effective selection method focuses on what the job really is, gets relevant information from a candidate, and provides a framework for making rational and fair decisions in the hiring process.

Sample Résumé Screening Worksheet

Company: _____

Position: _____

Date: _____ Time: _____

Rate each of the characteristics below according to the following scale:

    0 = does not meet expectations   1 = meets some expectations

    2 = meets expectations   3 = exceeds expectations

Name: _____

Education 0 1 2 3   Years of Experience 0 1 2 3

Supervisory Experience 0 1 2 3   Professional Development 0 1 2 3

Demonstrated Interpersonal Skills 0 1 2 3

Other _____ 0 1 2 3

TOTAL SCORE _____

Name: _____

Education 0 1 2 3   Years of Experience 0 1 2 3

Supervisory Experience 0 1 2 3   Professional Development 0 1 2 3

Demonstrated Interpersonal Skills 0 1 2 3

Other _____ 0 1 2 3

TOTAL SCORE _____

Name: _____

Education 0 1 2 3   Years of Experience 0 1 2 3

Supervisory Experience 0 1 2 3   Professional Development 0 1 2 3

Demonstrated Interpersonal Skills 0 1 2 3

Other _____ 0 1 2 3

TOTAL SCORE _____

Name: _____

Education 0 1 2 3   Years of Experience 0 1 2 3

Supervisory Experience 0 1 2 3   Professional Development 0 1 2 3

Demonstrated Interpersonal Skills 0 1 2 3

Other _____ 0 1 2 3

TOTAL SCORE _____

Why can't I just review the résumés and pick those who have the most years of service or excellent experience?

The main reason is that most résumés are not worth the paper they are printed on or the bytes in cyberspace they occupy. When a candidate says they have 20 years' experience doing something, that statement does not imply anything about their competency for the last 20 years. Likewise, a person who says that he led his department to a 30 percent increase in sales is not necessarily a great manager if he also shares with you the fact that he had 50 percent more sales staff. Some associations you need to commit to memory when reviewing résumés are:

Experience ≠ Accomplishment
Education ≠ Competency
A Given Responsibility or Activity ≠ Positive Result

The easiest way to determine if a statement on a résumé is worth anything is to put the words "and it cost my company thousands of dollars" after it and see if the statement still makes sense. For example:

(1) Résumé states:
"Implemented a new accounting system" you add,
"and it cost my company thousands of dollars."

The statement makes sense; therefore, it does not tell you anything useful about the candidate's performance.

(2) Résumé States:
"Opened three new sales territories and increased profitability by 25 percent." You add,

"and it cost my company thousands of dollars."

The statement does not make sense; therefore, it does tell you that the candidate's actions had a positive impact on the company.

Be particularly suspicious when a candidate talks about teamwork because the focus needs to be on his or her specific accomplishments within the team.

In general, the three significant parts of the résumé are the contact information, education and special skills, and work experience that demonstrates specific accomplishments. Rating these factors on a worksheet in a systematic fashion will give you the ability to look at all the applicants on a level playing field, and then choose only the best to continue in the selection process. Unnecessary testing and interviewing is a waste of everyone's time and resources, and, let's face it, none of us really relishes this phase of the process to begin with. The following is your best guide to pre-employment testing and interviewing.

PRE-EMPLOYMENT TESTING

Tests or procedures used to measure an individual's employment or career-related qualifications and interests are considered personnel assessment tools. These tools include traditional knowledge and ability tests, inventories, subjective procedures and projective instruments. The various instruments available have different uses and applications; it is important to determine what exactly you want to test and why before deciding on an assessment tool.

- What is the purpose of the tool; i.e., selection, placement, promotion, career counseling or training?

- What is it designed to measure; i.e., abilities, skills, work styles, work values or vocational interests?

- What is it designed to predict; i.e., job performance, managerial potential, career success, job satisfaction or tenure?

- What format does it come in; i.e., paper-and-pencil, work-sample or computer simulation?

- What is the level of standardization, objectivity and quantifiability (some tools are fully standardized and have proven predictive ability; others, like personality inventories, are more subjective with no specific right or wrong answers)?

Types of Pre-Employment Tests

People differ on many psychological and physical characteristics; tests, inventories and procedures are assessment tools that can be used to measure these individual abilities, values and personality traits. The most common types of assessment tools include the following:

Mental and Physical Ability Tests

When properly applied, ability tests are among the most useful and valid tools available for predicting success in jobs and training across a wide variety of occupations. Ability tests are most commonly used for entry-level jobs and applicants without professional training or advanced degrees.

Mental ability tests are generally used to measure the ability to learn and perform particular job responsibilities. Examples of some mental abilities are verbal, quantitative and spatial. Physical ability tests usually encompass abilities such as strength, endurance and flexibility.

- General ability tests typically measure one or more broad mental abilities, such as verbal, mathematical and reasoning skills.

- Specific ability tests include measures of distinct physical and mental abilities, such as reaction time, written comprehension, mathematical reasoning and mechanical ability, that are important for many jobs and occupations. For example, good mechanical ability may be important for success in auto mechanic and engineering jobs; physical endurance may be critical for fire-fighting jobs.

When using ability testing, it is important to consider discriminatory impacts: Mental abilities tests may adversely impact some racial minority groups—if speed is a component of the test, older workers may be adversely impacted; physical ability tests often result in adverse impact against women and older persons.

Achievement Tests

Achievement tests, also known as proficiency tests, are frequently used to measure an individual's current knowledge or skills that are important to a particular job. These tests generally fall into one of the following formats:

- Knowledge tests typically involve specific questions to determine how much the individual knows about particular job tasks and responsibilities.

- Work-sample or performance tests require the individual to actually demonstrate or perform one or more job tasks. These tests, by their makeup, generally show a high degree of job-relatedness.

Biodata Inventories

Biodata inventories are standardized questionnaires that gather job-relevant biographical information, such as amount and type of schooling, job experiences and hobbies. They are generally used to predict job and training performance, tenure and turnover. They capitalize on the well-proven notion that past behavior is a good predictor of future behavior.

Personality Inventories

In addition to abilities, knowledge and skills, job success also depends on an individual's personal characteristics. Personality inventories designed for use in employment contexts are used to evaluate such characteristics as motivation, conscientiousness, self-confidence or how well an employee might get along with fellow workers. Research has shown that, in certain situations, use of personality tests with other assessment instruments can yield helpful predictions. Since there are usually no right or wrong answers to the test items, test-takers may provide socially desirable answers. However, sophisticated personality inventories often have "lie-scales" built in, which allow such response patterns to be detected.

Honesty and Integrity Measures

Honesty tests are a specific type of personality test and they are broadly categorized into two types:

- Overt integrity tests gauge involvement in and attitudes toward theft and employee delinquency. Test items typically ask for opinions about frequency and extent of employee theft, leniency or severity of attitudes toward theft, and rationalizations of theft. They also include direct questions about admissions of, or dismissal for, theft or other unlawful activities.

- Personality-based measures typically contain disguised-purpose questions to gauge a number of personality traits. These traits are usually associated with a broad range of counterproductive employee behaviors, such as insubordination, excessive absenteeism, disciplinary problems and substance abuse.

If you choose to use an honesty test to select people for a particular job, you should document the business necessity of such a test. This would require a detailed job analysis, including an assessment of the consequences of hiring a dishonest individual. A number of states currently have statutes restricting the use of honesty and integrity measures; consult regulations in your area that govern the use of these tests before using them.

Medical Examinations

Medical examinations are used to determine if a person can safely and adequately perform a specific job. Administering medical exams to job applicants or asking questions related to disability prior to making a job offer is prohibited. Once you make a job offer to an applicant, you may require a medical exam as long as you require the exam of all persons entering the same job category. You may require a medical exam even if it bears no relevance to job performance. However, if you refuse to hire based on the results of the medical exam, the reasons for refusing to hire must be founded on issues of job-relevance and business necessity.

Drug and Alcohol Tests

An employer may prohibit the use of alcohol and illegal drugs at the workplace and may require that employees not be under the influence of either while on the job. Some commonly reported negative work behaviors and outcomes associated with alcohol and drug abuse are industrial accidents, work-related injuries, excessive absenteeism or tardiness and workplace violence. If your organization uses drug or alcohol tests to make personnel decisions, you should develop a written policy governing such a program to ensure compliance with all relevant federal, state and local laws. Most states require written consent of employees and applicants before drug or alcohol tests can be administered. Consult the ADA, the EEOC Technical Assistance Manual on the Employment Provisions of the Americans with Disabilities Act, the EEOC ADA Enforcement Guidance: Pre-employment Disability-Related Questions and Medical Examinations, and the EEOC Uniform Guidelines on Employee Selection Procedures, as well as your state and local laws when developing a drug- or alcohol-testing program.

Examples of commonly used pre-employment tests are General Aptitude Test Battery (GATB), Differential Aptitude Tests (DAT), Watson-Glaser Critical Thinking Appraisal, Personnel Tests for Industry, Bennett Mechanical Comprehension Test, Myers-Briggs Typology, Clerical Abilities Battery, Fundamental Interpersonal Relations Orientation-Behavior (FIRO-B), and many other specialized tests developed by companies specializing in human resource assessment.

Why Test?

The most common reasons for using pre-employment testing in the selection process are:

- Current selection or placement procedures result in poor hiring decisions.

- Employee productivity is low.

- Employee errors have serious financial, health or safety consequences.

- There is high employee turnover or absenteeism.

- Present assessment procedures do not meet current legal and professional standards.

Professionally developed tests and procedures that are used as part of a planned assessment program may help you select and hire more qualified and productive employees. However, it is essential to understand that all assessment tools are subject to errors, both in measuring a characteristic, such as verbal ability, and in predicting performance criteria, such as success on the job. This is true for all tests and procedures, regardless of how objective or standardized they might be.

- Do not expect any test or procedure to measure a personal trait or ability with perfect accuracy for every single person.

- Do not expect any test or procedure to be completely accurate in predicting performance.

There will be cases where a test score or procedure will predict someone to be a good worker, who, in fact, is not. There will also be cases where an individual receiving a low score will be rejected, who, in fact, would actually be capable and a good worker. Because of these selection errors, it is important to remember that testing is only one of many ways to assess a candidate's abilities, and judgment needs to be exercised when applying test results.

Principles of Assessment
To minimize selection error, it is important to apply the following principles:

1. **Use assessment tools in a purposeful manner.** As an employer, you must first be clear about what you want to accomplish with your assessment program in order to select the proper tools to achieve those goals. Only use tests that are appropriate for your particular purpose.

2. **Use the whole-person approach to assessment.**

An assessment instrument may provide you with important employment-related information about an individual; however, no assessment tool is 100 percent reliable or valid, therefore pre-employment tests should be only one part of a comprehensive selection process.

3. **Use only assessment instruments that are unbiased and fair to all groups.** Using unbiased and fair tests will help you select a qualified and diverse workforce. Review the fairness evidence associated with assessment instruments before selecting tools by examining the test manual and independent test reviews.

4. **Use only reliable assessment instruments and procedures.** A reliable instrument will provide accurate and consistent scores. This means that if a person takes the same test again and again, he or she should get similar scores each time. To meaningfully interpret test scores and make useful career- or employment-related decisions, use only reliable tools.

5. **Use only valid assessment procedures and instruments.** Validity refers to the characteristic the assessment instrument measures and how well the instrument measures that characteristic. For example, a test that may be valid for predicting someone's "job knowledge," may not be valid for predicting his or her "leadership skills." You must be sure that the instrument is valid for the purpose for which it is to be used.

6. **Use assessment tools that are appropriate for the target population.** An assessment tool is usually developed for use with a specific group; it may not be valid for other groups. Tests should be appropriate for your target population and need to consider such factors as reading levels, cultural backgrounds and language barriers.

7. **Use assessment instruments for which understandable and comprehensive documentation is available.** Are the instructions for administration and interpretation understandable? Is the information sufficiently comprehensive to evaluate the suitability of the instrument for your needs? Test manuals should cover test development, psychometric characteristics, procedures for administration, scoring and interpretation, and the recommended uses of the instrument.

8. **Ensure that administration staff are properly trained.** Assessment instruments must be administered properly to obtain valid results. Administrators should be given ample time to learn their responsibilities and should practice by administering tests to other staff before administering tests to applicants. Some test publishers may run training sessions for test administration and interpretation.

9. **Ensure that testing conditions are suitable for all test-takers.** Staff should ensure that the testing environment is suitable and that administration

procedures are uniform for all test-takers.

10. **Provide reasonable accommodation in the assessment process for people with disabilities.** To ensure that qualified individuals with disabilities have an equal chance to demonstrate their potential, accommodations in the assessment process may be necessary. For example, if administering a Braille version of a test, allowing extra time to complete the test or supplying a reader may be appropriate. Use the level of accommodation appropriate to your workplace as a guide to the level of accommodation allowed for the test.

11. **Maintain assessment instrument security.** All materials used in the assessment process must be kept secure.

12. **Maintain confidentiality of assessment results.** Assessment results are highly personal and employers must respect the test-taker's right to confidentiality. Assessment results should only be shared with those who have a legitimate need to know.

13. **Ensure that scores are interpreted properly.** Tests are used to make inferences about people's characteristics, capabilities and future performance. Ensure that there is solid evidence to justify your test score interpretations and the employment decisions you make based on those scores. The test manual should provide instructions on how to properly interpret test results.

Can a good pre-employment test replace traditional hiring procedures, such as interviewing or checking references? The short answer: NO!

The tests are not designed to replace good interviewing and a comprehensive selection process; they are, however, designed to provide additional information that can be used to make a more accurate hiring decision. As the business market becomes more competitive, companies are well advised to consider pre-employment tests in order to stay ahead in the business of hiring.

INTERVIEWING

The Purpose of Interviewing

The main reason we conduct employment interviews is to predict performance. By the end of the interview, we want to predict, as accurately as possible, whether or not the candidate in front of us can and will do the job. But that is just the first step because all people are different; they have different aptitudes, capabilities, attitudes and dispositions, so even people with the same skill set will approach situations differently, have different preferences and behave uniquely. This means that even though a person may have the requisite skills and knowledge to do the job, he or she may not be inclined or motivated to do it so they will not do the job well. For this reason interviews must go beyond whether the person can do the job and determine whether or not the person will do a good job.

Traditional Interviewing

Traditionally, interviews have focused on an applicant's

education, qualifications and experience. If an applicant meets the educational requirements, has the desired experience, appears to have the desired personal characteristics and responds appropriately (or as expected) to the questions, then the person is judged qualified for the job. The problem is that if you screened your applications properly, you should only be interviewing people who are on the surface "qualified" to do the job, thus the interview process needs to dig deeper and determine if the person will do the job well. To determine this, we use the most important rule of human behavior:

The best predictor of future
performance is past performance.

So, the best way to determine whether or not a person will do a good job at your company is to determine what kind of job they did in their last position, or in school, or in whatever capacity is relevant to their circumstances. This means that instead of asking someone how they work in teams, you ask them to recall for you a time when they worked as part of a team and what their contribution was.

For example: Bob is interviewing Mary for a position as an Administrative Assistant. His business is expanding rapidly so he needs someone to help him with all aspects of administration from answering phones to preparing correspondence to tracking purchase orders and invoices; essentially this person will be his "go-to" person for all administrative duties. Mary has 15 years' experience in administration; she has worked for two companies as a Receptionist, an Accounts Payable Clerk, and an Executive Secretary. Bob is very excited about her skill set and is sure she will be able to keep his company organized and running smoothly.

Traditional Interview

Q: **"What were your duties in your last job?"**

A: "Well, I would say I ran the ship. My boss was a very busy man so I took care of the office for him. I organized his filing systems, I made sure suppliers were paid on time and I kept on top of our receivables. I wrote all of my boss's letters and faxes, and filtered his e-mail for him; I tried to make his job as easy as possible for him. If it's administrative, I can do it."

Q: **"What are your strengths and weaknesses?"**

A: "My strengths are my ability to organize, my attention to detail, and my communication skills. I guess a weakness would be that I tend to be a perfectionist; I always want to do my best."

Q: **"What were the most and least enjoyable aspects of your last job?**

A: "I loved the autonomy and responsibility I was given. My boss trusted me to get things done and that's exactly what I did. If you tell me to get something done, you don't have to worry about it because I will do it. There really wasn't anything in particular I didn't like about my last job. There was a lot of unnecessary "water-cooler" talk on Monday mornings and Friday afternoons but that is just to be expected."

Q: **"How do you make use of your spare time?"**

A: [laughing] "What spare time? I wish I knew what that was, but I can always find something that needs to be done. I'm an organizer so I never seem to run out of things to do."

Q: **"How would other people describe you?"**

A: "People are always saying how dedicated I am and how I only give my 100 percent best. I'm very motivated and I enjoy a challenge. Your office will run like a well-oiled machine with me in charge of administration."

Q: **"What is your approach to teamwork?"**

A: "Working as a team is so important these days because you're only as strong as your weakest link. I love to help my coworkers, that way we all get things done more efficiently. I work well independently too, but working as part of a team makes me feel like I'm really part of the organization."

I'm sure most, if not all, of those questions are ones you have asked, or have been asked, in your interviewing history. They are very typical questions designed to get the interviewee to tell us more about themselves and help us get an idea of their motivations and personality. From the sounds of it, Mary is an ideal Administrative Assistant for Bob; she will be able to get in there and organize his office, take care of things and keep on top of the office functions. She certainly has the right attitude about working independently and as part of a team, and who doesn't want their office systems organized perfectly? This is a no-brainer: Mary is hired.

Hold on: It isn't quite that clear-cut, because although Mary has told us some wonderful things about what she has done, we have no evidence to confirm that what she did was advantageous to the company. When we ask someone to describe what he or she did, we often assume that if the person did it, they must have done it well: this is often not the case! Let's look at the same interview using a behavioral approach to the questions.

Behavioral Interviewing

The basic principle underlying a behavioral interview is:
The best predictor of future performance is past performance in similar situations. More specifically:

- The more recent the past behavior, the greater is predictive power.

- The more long-standing the behavior, the greater its predictive power.

Behavioral interviewing focuses on past performance. By focusing on past performance, this interview method greatly increases your ability to predict whether or not a person will be the "top performer" for which your organization is looking. With a behavioral approach, we go beyond the traditional question and probe for details about a specific time when a desired work characteristic was demonstrated. For instance, rather than asking a person how they approach teamwork, we ask them about a time when they worked as a team and get them to describe their exact involvement. There are four types of information gathered in an interview, and not all the information is of equal value to the interviewer.

Technical/Credential Questions

These questions ask about specific knowledge, education, past achievements, etc., and all of the information is verifiable.

- What degree(s) do you hold?
- What size of budget did you manage?
- Do you have a driver's license?

Advantages	Disadvantages
Provide clues to whether an applicant does have the knowledge his or her credentials indicate.	Gives a good idea about whether the person can do the job but doesn't allow us to predict whether or not the person will do the job or do it well.

These are great screening questions that should be answered before the interview stage, either through résumé screening, phone calls or testing. If a person does not meet your required minimums, the interview is not the place to find out.

Experience Questions

These questions ask about specific activities the applicant has done in the past and they provide a solid overview of the applicant's skill set.

- For what were you responsible at your last job?

- When you have a conflict with a coworker, how do you handle it?

- How do you deal with stress?

Advantages	Disadvantages
These questions provide an overview of what has been done in the past and are a helpful guide to probing for more specific information about performance.	By themselves, these questions do not provide information about the quality of the applicant's performance. We may assume if the person did it, they did it well; that is often not the case.

These questions are good starting points, but without more specific information, you will not get any information about how well the person did in the situation or how they will likely behave in the future.

Opinion Questions
These questions get the applicant to self-evaluate and tell you what they think about a given topic and you get an idea about what is important to the person.

- What are your strengths and weaknesses?

- If your boss handed you four assignments all due by the end of the day and you already had a huge in-basket, what would you do?

- Describe your ideal work environment.

Advantages	Disadvantages
These questions may provide information about what the person thinks is important and allow for further probing as it relates to the job opening.	These answers do not provide any real evidence about what the candidate actually does/will do in a given situation. Most applicants will be able to answer these questions the way the interviewer expects them to be answered.

When we ask opinion questions, we forget that just because a person says something, that does not mean it is true. An interviewee can tell you, hypothetically speaking, that if their workload became unmanageable they would calmly approach their boss, explain the situation and work with him or her to prioritize the ongoing assignments. The answer is textbook perfect, but it sheds no light on the fact that the last time they got behind a little and the boss asked them to stay late, they shouted "Workplace exploitation." from the top of their lungs in the cafeteria and went to the media claiming sweat-shop conditions abound. Beware: People with a good dose of common sense and the ability to think quickly do very well with opinion questions!

Behavioral Questions

These questions are detailed accounts of specific events from the applicant's past.

- In our organization, we often work as teams. Please tell me about the most significant contribution you were able to make as a team member.

- Catching problems early can save a lot of time and

money. Think about a time when you noticed the early warning signs of a problem that would have been costly if not detected.

Advantages	Disadvantages
Allows the interviewer to objectively assess the candidate's qualifications yielding accurate hiring decisions. It is almost as if the interviewer is watching the candidate perform in the workplace. People enjoy telling what they have done; especially top performers who are grateful for the opportunity to describe their accomplishments.	Behavioral interviewing takes time and practice. Interviewers require more skill and effort to ask behavioral questions well.

By now it should be obvious that there is a better way to ask questions — that better way is called behavioral interviewing. Behavioral interviewing goes one step beyond the experience and opinion questions and asks for a detailed account of a specific event from the applicant's past. Why? Because the best predictor of future behavior is past behavior!

All four types of interview questions appear in behavioral interviews but to varying degrees. In behavioral interviews, the focus shifts from opinion and experiences to actual examples of past behavior. These actual examples are then fully explored so the interviewer can get detailed answers to his or her questions. The candidate is also asked to provide a reference (person who witnessed the situation or can comment on it) if possible, and the interviewer has the option to verify the information by getting the reference's perspective on the candidate's performance in that situation.

The focus of any question can be modified to fit a behavioral framework with some additional probing about specific situations:

> **Q: "What do you think are your strengths as an employee?**
> A: "I'm a very dependable and reliable worker."

The traditional interviewer would take that information at face value and form a high opinion of the applicant; the behavioral interviewer would want some proof of the person's dependability, so they would ask for a specific example.

> **Q: "Can you describe a time when you demonstrated dependability?"**
> A: "Sure, last week my boss had an early breakfast meeting so I opened up the shop for him. I arrived 30 minutes early to make sure everything was ready (lights, heat, photocopier, etc.) for when the rest of the employees arrived. I did such a great job that I'll be opening up Monday, Wednesday and Friday from now on—at least until I get this job!"

By taking the question to the next level, you gain valuable information about the person, and you can safely predict that they will behave similarly in future situations.

Let's take a look at Bob's interview of Mary using a behavioral approach this time:

Q: **"What were your duties in your last job?"**

A: "Well, I would say I ran the ship. My boss was a very busy
man so I took care of the office for him. I organized his filing
systems, I made sure suppliers were paid on time, and I kept
on top of our receivables. I wrote all of my boss's letters and
faxes, and filtered his e-mail for him; I tried to make his job
as easy as possible for him. If it's administrative, I can do it."
[Sounds like a strong, take-charge person.]

Q: **That's great, sounds like you're a take-charge kind of
person. Tell me about a time, though, when you "bit off
a little more than you could chew."**

A: Well, uh, there was this one time when I took it upon myself
to collect on an outstanding receivable. I'd heard Jerry, my
boss, talking to his partner about some financial difficulty,
and I knew that this one company owed us a bunch of money
so I made a few phone calls demanding payment and sent a
demand letter. I'd done that in the past on Jerry's request so
I knew I was within our legal requirements. The problem was
that Jerry and the owner of the company had already worked
out some arrangement between them and when the guy got
the demand letter, well, Jerry was left with lots of explaining
to do. In that case, my initiative got the better of me, but I
sure learned from the situation: get your boss's approval!"
[Hmm, maybe a little overzealous, but she's learned from the
experience.]

Q: **"What are your strengths and weaknesses?"**

A: "My strengths are my ability to organize, my attention to
detail, and my communication skills. I guess a weakness
would be that I tend to be a perfectionist—I always want to
do my best." [Perfectionism... that may mean less efficient.]

Q: "Tell me more about the project you felt you did most perfectly."

A: "That's easy: I reorganized all of Jerry's filing system. When I first got there it was a mess, but I never seemed to have any time to get in there and fix it up. As a surprise, when Jerry took vacation a couple of years ago, I redid everything—you've never seen a neater set of filing cabinets, not a file misplaced, all the papers in order, I tracked down missing invoices, you name it. If we ever need the information, it is at our fingertips." [Yikes! Red flag: perfectionism to the extreme!]

Q: "Wow, sounds like a lot of work. What was Jerry's reaction to his surprise?"

A: "He loved it and it made the data entry that much easier when we moved to an electronic system a few months later. It's a shame we didn't get to use the new system much before the changeover, but at least the files looked good for a little while." [Big red flag: she created her own project, spent an inordinate amount of time doing it and it was obsolete in a few months!]

Q: "We do a lot of teamwork here; can you tell me about a time when you worked as part of team and what your involvement was."

A: "Changing our records over to an electronic database was a team effort and I was in charge of it because I knew those files inside and out—I spent two weeks straight reorganizing them! Some other team members tried to help but they really didn't have the intimate knowledge of the system that I had, so the systems guy and I worked together really well and we got our new system up and running. My coworkers really appreciated me taking on the project and now if any of them have questions, they can come to me and I'll figure it out for them." [Flags all over the place: she wants to be in control instead taking the time to teach the new file system to her coworkers—not a team player!]

Q: **"What were the most and least enjoyable aspects of your last job?**
A: "I loved the autonomy and responsibility I was given. My boss trusted me to get things done and that's exactly what I did. If you tell me to get something done, you don't have to worry about it because I will do it. There really wasn't anything in particular I didn't like about my last job. There was a lot of unnecessary "water-cooler" talk on Monday mornings and Friday afternoons but that is just to be expected." [I bet you liked the autonomy—you wouldn't accept anything less!]

Q: **"How do you make use of your spare time?"**
A: [laughing] "What spare time? I wish I knew what that was, but I can always find something that needs to be done. I'm an organizer so I never seem to run out of things to do." [If it ain't broke, …]

Q: **"How would other people describe you?"**
A: "People are always saying how dedicated I am and how I only give my 100 percent best. I'm very motivated and I enjoy a challenge. Your office will run like a well-oiled machine with me in charge of administration." [Well, I don't think this machine is going to be run by you; who knows what side trips you'd take it on!]

The same basic interview questions lead to very different impressions of Mary and her ability to do the job. Her tendency to takeover and create her own work according to her priorities did not come across in the traditional interview, but with a few simple probes, it became obvious that Mary's idea of administrative excellence was a little too autocratic for Bob's liking.

TRADITIONAL VS. BEHAVIORAL INTERVIEWS

Behavioral, structured interviewing techniques are replacing traditional interviewing practices due to the high success of this technique in overcoming the typical interview problems:

- Inadequate job-relevant data.

- Interviewers asking the same questions.

- Misinterpretation of applicant information.

- Biases and stereotypes.

- Allowing one dimension to influence decisions.

- Allowing applicant to control the interview.

- Making hiring decisions too soon.

- Over-reliance on the interview.

- Disorganized interview.

- Telling instead of seeking information.

- Insufficient note-taking.

- Using different standards for selection.

Traditional hiring methods merely elicit responses that address credentials, opinions and feelings. Rarely will traditional interview questions prompt the candidate to tell the interviewer about an actual job performance or about job experiences and accomplishments in specific situations. Answers given by candidates do not focus on what a person actually did in a specific situation on a previous job, how it was done and under what circumstances it was done. As a result, traditional interviewing does a poor job of helping employers predict how a candidate will behave in specific situations.

This poor predictive ability has been repeatedly proven in many research studies.

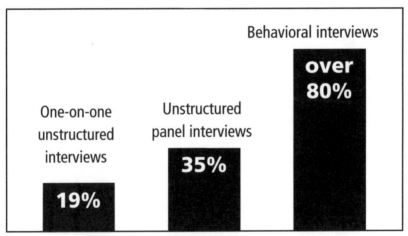

PERCENTAGE OF PREDICTIVE ACCURACY

| Comparison of Traditional vs. Behavioral/Structured ||
Traditional	Behavioral/Structured
Hit-and-miss data	Intentional coverage
Casual/Informal	Detailed agenda
Inadequate information	Job-relevant data
Single decision-maker	Collaborative decision
Overlap of information coverage	No overlap
Time-consuming	Efficient
Non-defensible	Audit trail

SETTING UP THE BEHAVIORAL INTERVIEW

When we interview people, our purpose is not to trip them up or make them unduly nervous or uncomfortable; our goal is to figure out if their particular set of skills, personality attributes and aptitudes are a good fit with our organization and the position for which they are applying. Because behavioral interviewing is challenging, it's hard to think of good examples when you're on the spot; it is particularly important to prepare the candidate for the type of interview questions they will encounter.

Make Personal Contact

Before the interview, call the candidate and discuss the interview process with him or her. You can glean a great deal of information about a person from a five-minute phone call, and it sets the tone for your formal meeting. Give them an example of the type of question you will be asking. You may even want them to fax or e-mail you a written response to one of your questions. Once you've received the answer, you can call back and schedule the exact date and time of your meeting. This simple sample will provide you with a wealth of information about how well the candidate follows directions, how quickly they grasp new concepts, how well they write and organize their thoughts, how motivated they are (did you receive the answer in hours or days or weeks?), etc. Plus, that's one less interview question you have to ask so you've saved yourself time and money already.

Prepare Your Questions

Have a prepared set of questions ready that you will ask each candidate. This adds objectivity to the very subjective process of interviewing. You are much better able to compare candidates when you are working with similar information. Use your job descriptions to derive questions that address the key areas of competence related to the position. When looking for a graphic designer, you want to learn about the person's creativity level and capacity for original thinking; for a software technician, attention to detail is a key area for discussion; and you want to know how well your administrative assistant follows direction.

Many of the interview questions you create will be usable for other vacancies as they become available. The questions only need to be tweaked or a few specific ones created to customize the interview to a new opening. Behavioral factors that all interviews should address are:

- Communication

- Interpersonal skills

- Motivation

- Self-management

- Initiative

- Stress management

Technical competency questions will be tailored to each specific position and supervisors and managers should also address leadership, decision-making and management skills.

The following is a list of excellent interview questions gathered from a variety of sources. Some are written behaviorally and others can be adapted by asking for a specific example. All of the questions require the candidates to assess their past behavior and think introspectively.

Examples of Great Interview Questions
General/Introspective Questions

- "What do you feel are your greatest strengths?"

- "What is the best constructive criticism you've ever received?"

- "Describe the accomplishment you are most proud of."

- "What causes you to lose your temper?"

- "Would your supervisor be surprised that you are looking for another job?"

- "How would your coworkers and colleagues describe you?"

- "How would your friends describe you?"

- "What type of supervision brings out the best in you?"

- "What makes you stand out in front of your peers?"

- "Tell me about a time when you failed to accomplish an objective."

Communication and Interpersonal Skills Questions

- "Communication skills are important in this job; please tell me your two biggest strengths as a communicator."

- "Understanding someone else's needs is often required in this job; please tell me about the time when you probed beyond the obvious and you got the most rewarding result."

- "Trying to understand where other people are coming from is difficult, tell me about the time you were most frustrated trying to discover what somebody wanted or needed from you."

- "What is your biggest strength in dealing with people?"

- "Flexibility is important in this work environment. Please tell me about a time when you were most flexible in your job. Be very specific and describe one actual incident."

- "Tell me about a time when you had to make an unpopular decision."

- "Tell me about the time when you best handled an irate customer."

Teamwork

- "What has been your greatest accomplishment as a member of a team?"

- "Do you prefer working alone or in a group?"

- "When working in a group, what role do you prefer?"

- "Not every team runs smoothly. Tell me about a time when you found it most difficult to work as a team member."

- "Tell me about a time when your team disagreed with your ideas and how you handled it."

- "How would your teammates describe your style when working together?"

- "Tell me about the time when your boss contributed

the most to your team accomplishment."

- "Tell me about the time when your boss's involvement most hindered your team accomplishment."

Motivation

- "Now let's talk about what motivates you. Based on your experience, tell me two things that motivated you to do good work."

- "Please give me your best example of a time when you made the best use of discretionary (spare) time."

- "What kind of supervisor is likely to get the most out of you?"

- "What is the key difference between your performance when the boss is in the office and when he or she is away?"

- "Tell me about some things you've initiated that have added value to your job."

- "What is the best reward you've ever received?"

Problem-Solving/Creativity

- "Tell me about a time when you noticed a quality defect and you were able to correct it."

- "Sometimes, in spite of our best efforts, errors occur. Please describe a time when something slipped by you, resulting in the biggest problem."

- "I'd like you to recall a time when you suggested a change in a procedure or some other aspect of your job that achieved the best result."

- "In your last position, what projects did you give the highest priority and why?"

- "How do you organize yourself at work? Do you use an agenda, a day planner, lists, etc.?"

- "Tell me about a time when you persuaded someone to do something that had the best result."

- "Tell me about a time that your boss asked you to do something that you did not totally agree with."

Stress Management

- "Tell me about the tightest deadline you were able to meet."

- "Recall a time when you had too many projects on the go and your work quality suffered because of it."

- "Is honesty always the best policy?"

- "Let's say you've had a great day at work. When you go home and tell a loved one about it, what are you describing?"

- "Let's say you've had a horrible day at work. When you go home and tell a loved one about it, what are you describing?"

- "Recall a time when you were given very little time to make required changes to a project or a procedure."

Structure the Interview

Who Does the Interviewing?

It is absolutely critical that the person who will be supervising the new employee the most be included in, if not in charge of, the hiring process. Who better to assess a candidate's fit than the person who knows the intimate details of the department's functions, personalities and idiosyncrasies? This may seem obvious, but in far too many instances, it does not happen. The large corporation has a dedicated, professional recruitment staff that fill vacancies like a production line, sending the chosen few to meet their supervisor for the first on time on their first scheduled shift. Small-business owners often interview candidates for all positions, and then send the lucky candidate to meet their supervisor. Hiring is difficult enough without excluding the very people whose work lives are affected the most in the process.

To exacerbate the situation, many interviews are held in isolation. Interviewing is timely and costly, but the more relevant opinions you can gather about a candidate, the better your hiring decision will be. The "two heads are better than one" analogy has never been so true when it comes to interviewing. Just as all people are different, so are their perceptions of other people. To some interviewers, a candidate who has quick, intelligent responses to all the questions may seem perfect, and other, more cynical (or more experienced) interviewers will see that person as too perfect and too smooth; red flags that indicate further probing is needed. When hiring for technical positions, it is imperative that someone with a technical background be included to ensure the person can actually perform the various aspects of the job. While including a few key people in the interview process is important, it is equally important to not intimidate the candidates with a large number interviewers at one time. Large-panel interviewing is common for positions that operate in very stressful environments, but the average position does not require such extreme measures.

Rating the Responses
Dimensions to Rate

- **When:** When did the situation occur? Last week, last month, last year, last century?

- **Situation:** What took place? Describe the situation in detail.

- **Action:** What did the candidate do? Describe what the candidate actually did (or did not do).

- **Outcome:** What was the outcome? What happened as a result?

- **Reference:** Who witnessed the event? Can we use this person as a reference?

Answer Quality

Answers that are descriptors always take the past tense. They describe what the candidate did in a specific situation. Indicators of non-behavioral responses include the words: *should, could, would, may, will, sometimes, usually, always* and *often.*

Probe for Personal Accomplishments

Continually focus on the candidate's responses that include "I" and away from those that discuss "we." You need to discover what the candidate did personally and what outcomes resulted.

Tough Candidate Situations

The Silence

The candidate cannot think of an example.

- Allow the candidate time to think (15-second pause).

- Follow with a reassuring statement ("You're okay, keep thinking.").

- Rephrase the question.

The Bluff

The candidate denies being able to recall an example.

- For the, "It happens all the time" response, ask for the example that happened yesterday.

- For the "It was so long ago" response, say something like, "I realize it may be hard to remember all the details. Tell what you do remember."

The Slip

The candidate slips into giving an opinion.

- Compliment the candidate for the opinion, but probe for the most challenging example or specific incident.

- Assume responsibility for not phrasing the questions properly.

- Gently persist to get the example.

Always give the candidate ample opportunity to respond appropriately; if they can't, move on to the next question.

RATING GUIDELINES

With behavioral interviews, each candidate is asked the same question, but how do you come up with a systematic way to compare the different responses? There are probably as many ways to do this as there are interviewers, so the important point is to make sure you actually use a system. Some interviewers use a 5-point rating scale where each interviewer rates each response on a scale of 1 to 5. At the end, a total score is calculated and then final figures compared. A well-thought-out and well-articulated response that demonstrated a solid application of the concept being questioned would earn a score of 4 or 5. An applicant whose example is weak or demonstrates inappropriate application of a skill is given a 1 or 2. It may be necessary to give a candidate a zero if they cannot come up with an example after being provided with as much assistance as necessary.

Rating Scales

Questions that ask for a best example or achievement.	
Score	Criteria
0	Candidate could not provide an appropriate response to the question.
1 or 2	The answer is an example of a poorly planned or poorly executed behavior.
3	The answer is an example of a moderately planned or moderately executed behavior.
4 or 5	The answer is an example of a well-planned or well-executed behavior.

Questions that ask for the biggest disappointment or ineffective performance.	
Score	Criteria
0	Candidate could not provide an appropriate response to the question.
1 or 2	The example is a poorly planned, ineffective behavior with no improvement demonstrated.
3	The example is a moderately ineffective behavior with some improvement demonstrated.
4 or 5	The example demonstrates a novel problem that the candidate learned from and later demonstrated competence.

Some interviewers determine what the ideal candidate's responses are and then rate each interviewee depending on how similar their response is to the ideal one. This is problematic because it causes many interviewers to lead the interviewee toward the correct response. It is better to approach a question with no preconceived notions of an excellent answer; unconventional does not mean unsuitable just as predictable does not mean a prize. Other common rating errors to avoid are:

- **Elevation error.** Rating all candidates too high or too low.

- **Central tendency error.** Rating everyone in the middle of the scale.

- **Halo effect.** Rating all of a candidate's responses high because of one particularly impressive answer or characteristic.

HOW DO I BEGIN?

Set the candidate at ease. When it comes to the actual interview, try to set the person at ease as much as possible. One excellent way to do this is to give them a tour of the office or facility. Let them meet their potential coworkers and ask questions. Assess their level of friendliness, their interpersonal skills, their curiosity about the business; these first few minutes will speak volumes about how the candidates carry themselves and about how others perceive them. If you're hiring for a management position, you certainly want someone who relates well to all levels of employees in the organization; likewise, a potential receptionist should be relatively outgoing, and it would be nice if the computer programmer looked up from his or her notebook long enough to say hi .

Appoint a Leader

Before the interview, choose someone to lead the process. This person is responsible for keeping the interview on track and on time.

Prepare Interview Sheets

Make sure all interviewers have a copy of the questions. Determine the order of questions before the interview.

Structuring Statement

Begin the interview with a structuring statement that lets the applicant know what will happen in the interview and will put him or her at ease. This statement should address:

- Your background with the company.

- The position being interviewed for.

- The approximate length of the interview.

- Permission to take notes or tape-record the conversation.

- Recap of behavioral-based questions.

For example:

> "Well, let's start the process. I'm Harold Harried, the manager of Dewy, Cuttum & Howe Hair Salon, and this is Loretta Lopsitoff, our head stylist. We have prepared some questions for you to answer, and we'll be alternating between us, but feel free to direct your responses to either of us. The whole interview should take about 45 minutes, and then we'll give you an opportunity to ask questions of us. Some of our questions are quite insightful and will require you to provide specific examples of previous experiences; please feel free to take a few moments to formulate your idea, silence does not bother us—we want you to give us your best answer, so take your time. We'd like to take notes of your responses, is that all right? Great, let's begin."

Take Notes

Each interviewer should keep notes and rate each response as it is given. Use a predetermined rating scale like the one previously shown.

Close the Interview

Tell the candidate that the questions are finished, and invite him or her to ask you questions. Thank the candidate for their time and candor. Let the candidate know what to expect for the remainder of the process, when will a decision be made, how they can contact you, etc.

Reach a Consensus

After the interview, share the information and your rating with the other interviewers and reach a consensus on each dimension. This final rating is used to compare candidates.

SAMPLE BEHAVIORAL INTERVIEW

Bottling Technician—Interview

Candidate: _____ Date: _____

Interviewers: _____

_____

1. Let's begin by discussing any specific experience or licenses and certificates you have that are relevant to this job.

2. Briefly describe your duties in your last job.

3. Highly effective bottling technicians routinely monitor their own work for quality control. Tell me about a time when you noticed a quality defect and how you were able to correct it. When

    Situation

    Action

    Outcome

Reference

RATING: 0   1   2   3   4   5

4.   Sometimes, in spite of our best efforts, errors occur. Please
     describe a time when something slipped by you resulting in
     the biggest problem.
     When

     Situation

     Action

     Outcome

     Reference

     RATING: 0   1   2   3   4   5

5.   Communication skills are important in this job. Please tell me
     your two biggest strengths as a communicator.

6.   Bottling technicians need to communicate with all the people with which they work. Please tell me about a time when you used excellent communication skills to fully understand a coworker or customer.
When

Situation

Action

Outcome

Reference

RATING: 0   1   2   3   4   5

7.   Trying to understand others' needs can be difficult. Tell me about a time you were most frustrated trying to discover what somebody needed or wanted from you.
When

Situation

Action

Outcome

Reference

RATING: 0   1   2   3   4   5

8.   The next area of interest to us in interpersonal behavior. What is your biggest strength in dealing with people?

9.   In our organization, we often work as teams. Please tell me about the most significant contribution you were able to make as a team member.
When

Situation

Action

Outcome

Reference

RATING: 0   1   2   3   4   5

10. Not every team runs smoothly. Tell me about a time when you found it most difficult to work as a team member.

When

Situation

Action

Outcome

Reference

RATING: 0   1   2   3   4   5

11. Now let's talk about what motivates you. Based on your experience, tell me two things that motivated you to do good work.

12. Occasionally bottling technicians have discretionary (spare) time to fill. Please give me your best example of a time when you made the best use of discretionary (spare) time.
When

Situation

Action

Outcome

Reference

RATING: 0   1   2   3   4   5

13. Let's discuss your thinking abilities. Please tell me your strengths in the areas of thinking and problem-solving.

14. It is important for bottling technicians to be alert and identify areas for process improvement. I'd like you to recall a time when you suggested a change in a procedure or some other aspect of your job that achieved the best result.

When

Situation

Action

Outcome

Reference

RATING: 0   1   2   3   4   5

Thank you. That is all the questions we have for you. Do you have any questions you would like to ask?

THE PROFESSIONAL INTERVIEWEE

An entire industry has emerged that provides professional services to job seekers; from preparing expert résumés to coaching people through the interview process, there are a generation of savvy, professional job applicants. These people know all about behavioral interviewing and have been drilled on coming up with strong examples from their work history that demonstrate core competencies like teamwork, communication, conflict resolution, decision-making, problem-solving, time management, communication, and initiative that most companies are looking for. How do you determine if the person sitting in front of you is truly an industrious top performer or just a well-rehearsed interviewee? To avoid being fooled, you must make it clear to the candidate that you intend to check the validity of the examples they provide and that you will be doing thorough reference checks; this decreases the amount of deception enormously.

Getting Truthful Responses

It is important to ask candidates upfront who they will be providing as references. You want to know this information before you start asking them behavioral questions because if they give you a set of examples from a workplace that they are not providing a contact for, you have no way of knowing if the scenarios they describe are embellished or even real. When you ask a behavioral question add, "That's a great example; is there someone at the organization that I can contact who will be able to give me their perspective on the situation?" When candidates realize you aren't just going to take their word for it, their responses are more likely to be accurate and truthful.

Another important thing to remember when interviewing is to continuously probe for more information. This veers the conversation away from the rehearsed scenarios that the candidate is expecting and requires them to think on their feet. This ad-hoc style will improve the legitimacy of the answers given, and it allows you to see how the person responds under pressure. When venturing off the interview agenda, it is critical that you don't lead the applicant to the answer you want. Don't provide clues about what experience you're looking for and never ask a candidate if they have done this or that. Their automatic response will be, "Of course" or "Are you kidding, I love to do that!" Getting through the polish of the professional is difficult, and some professional interviewees may be perfect for your vacancy, but by continually mixing-it-up you will elicit more truthful and real responses.

Ask a Silly Question...

As well prepared as your questions are and as well prepared as the interviewers are, in the interview room, you must still be prepared for anything and everything! There are many seemingly intelligent, perfectly suitable candidates who slip through the cracks and respond to your questions in the most outrageous ways or do the most bizarre things. It will happen and it may be near impossible to keep a straight face, but while your mind is saying, "Next!" feign interest and concentration, document the answer and then file it away.

Kids say the darnedest things and so do interviewees; here's a collection of real tales:

- After answering the first few questions, a candidate

picked up his cell phone and called his parents to let them know the interview was going well.

- While discussing the candidate's interests, she offered to do an in-office demonstration: her interest was knife-throwing and she just happened to have her knives with her!

- At the end of the interview, a candidate expressed her interest in getting the position, but only if her boyfriend liked the company and the hiring manager. She then said, "He's waiting outside. Can I bring him in to say hello?"

- A candidate entered the lobby and identified herself to the receptionist. She then pulled two pairs of shoes from her bag and said, "Before the interviewer comes out, tell me which pair you think I should wear with this suit."

- When told she would be meeting with another interviewer, the candidate said, "Wait just a minute." She then took out a large bag from her briefcase and proceeded to reapply her makeup and hairspray, all in the first interviewer's office.

- When asked by the hiring manager why she was leaving her current job, the applicant said, "My manager is a jerk. All managers are jerks."

- When asked what the candidate was currently earning, she replied, "I really don't see how that is any of your business."

- After being complimented on his choice of college and the grade point average he achieved, the candidate replied, "I'm glad that got your attention. I didn't really go there."

- When asked by the hiring manager if he had any questions for him, the candidate replied by telling a knock-knock joke.

- An applicant said he was so well-qualified that if he didn't get the job, it would prove that the company's management was incompetent.

- One candidate wore a Walkman and said she could listen to the interviewer and the music at the same time.

- A candidate asked to see the interviewer's résumé to see if the personnel executive was qualified to judge her.

- An applicant said if he were hired, he would demonstrate his loyalty by having the corporate logo tattooed on his forearm.

- An interviewee pulled out a Polaroid camera and snapped a flash picture of the interviewer saying he collected photos of everyone who interviewed him.

- While the interviewer took a long-distance phone call, the applicant took out a copy of Penthouse, and looked through the photos only, stopping longest at the centerfold.

- During the interview, an alarm clock went off from the candidate's briefcase. He took it out, shut it off, apologized and said he had to leave for another interview.

- In the middle of answering a question, the applicant took off his right shoe and sock, removed a medicated foot powder from his briefcase and dusted it on the foot and in the shoe. While he was putting back the shoe and sock, he said that he had to use the powder four times a day, and this was the time.

Reference Checks

After you've carefully received many referenced work examples, the onus is on you to follow up and actually do the checking! No one likes reference-checking, and in this litigious day and age, you're more often than not going to be met with a "rank, file and serial number" response that confirms the person worked at the workplace from such a time to such a time and that is it. But, if you are armed with a specific incident that the candidate has given you and you are requesting confirmation of what actually transpired, you're much more likely to get in the door. The supervisor, manager, coworker or whoever you are talking to is put at ease by the fact that the candidate has already given you some inside information. What you want the reference to do is explain the scenario from their perspective and make sure that the candidate was not exaggerating their role, taking undue credit for something, or out and out fabricating an example.

Beyond confirming a scenario, reference checks are also the best way to get firsthand information about how the candidate conducts himself or herself in the workplace. Let's face it, people lose most of their humility when writing a résumé or giving an interview. Suddenly, all of their achievements are akin to splitting the atom and there is nothing they can't do. This is why objective, third-party information is needed to help make a hiring decision.

What to Ask

At a minimum, the reference check should include:

- Verification of employment dates.
- Verification of position or title held.
- Eligibility status for rehire.
- Reason for separation.
- Recommendation for another position/role.

This information will give you a sense of whether the person has been upfront with you and what kind of lasting impression they made on their previous employer. Obviously, people who are not considered eligible for rehire left under unfavorable circumstances; perhaps the reasoning came up in the interview, but if the candidate led you to believe everything was rosy, then this is a cause for red flags. The following is a very standard reference-check guide and is useful for most entry-level, technical and administrative positions.

REFERENCE-CHECK GUIDE

1. How long have you known/supervised the candidate?

2. What was his/her position and main job responsibilities?

3. Confirmation of employment dates.

4. What were his/her strengths?

5. Were there any areas that needed improvement?

6. How well did he/she get along with:
    Management
    Good   Fair   Poor

    Coworkers
    Good   Fair   Poor

    Clients/Customers
    Good   Fair   Poor

7. Would you describe this person as being people- or technologically oriented?

8. Did he/she require close supervision?

9. Describe his/her written and oral communication skills?

10. How satisfied were you with his/her time management skills?

REFERENCE-CHECK GUIDE (CONTINUED)

11. How satisfied were you with his/her punctuality and attendance?

12. What would you say motivates this person to do a job well?

13. How was his/her attitude towards their work?

14. What kind of work environment and position would this person thrive in?

15. Why did he/she leave your company?

16. Was proper notice given?

17. Would this person be eligible for a rehire with your company?

When hiring at a professional or executive level, you will want to include a discussion of the candidate's demonstrated capabilities in the following areas of core competency:

- Leadership

- Oral communication

- Written communication

- Long-term planning

- Short-term planning

- Managerial skills

- Decision-making

- Productivity

- Employee relations

- Budget administration

- Technical skills

- Integrity

- Crisis management

- Interpersonal relations

- Overall performance

For the executive, you will also want to inquire about the candidate's ability to attract and mentor management staff and confirm their last level of compensation.

How to Ask It

More often than not, references do not want to be caught in a defamation suit over something they may have said about a former employee. Many human resource and legal departments advise their employees to simply confirm dates of employment, position held and compensation level. Here are some tips to try to get the most out of your reference-check conversation.

Ask Targeted Questions

Use information you've obtained about specific incidents and be prepared to discuss the examples the candidate gave in the interview. If you ask a question about an applicant's strengths and weaknesses without reference to a specific incident, you are more likely to get generalities and personal opinions about the candidate; when you ask for specifics, you will get specifics in return.

Obtain Written Releases

Have the candidate give you written authorization to contact former employers, and have the form release both you and the former employers from any legal liability based on information obtained during the check. Prior to a reference check, fax or mail the candidate's written waiver and authorization to conduct the check. This will give the previous employer your name, position and telephone number, and it establishes good faith.

Document All Reference Responses

Keep an accurate written record of all the reference discussions to support your hiring decisions. Even if you only get the minimum verification of position held, employment dates and salary, this will show you at least attempted to check the candidate's references.

Wherever Possible, Meet in Person

There is no rule saying a reference check has to be conducted over the telephone. People are much less apt to lie or tell half-truths if they have to look you in the eye. There is also the power of non-verbal communication to consider; crossed arms, fidgeting and nervous glances are all subtle signs of deception or discomfort that you wouldn't pick up on the phone.

INTERNAL PROMOTION

In any organization, movement within the company is a key issue for many employees. The opportunity for advancement may be a key factor in finding and recruiting talent. Middle management is a vital role; they are the link between executive strategy and the employees who will carry out goals. Considering this central function, your strategy for hiring them speaks volumes on how you see the human resources in your organization as a whole.

- Do you value your people enough to take a chance on them?

- Do you hire entry-level positions with an eye to their promotional capability?

- Do you choose to promote from within or recruit from the outside?

When you choose to promote from within, you are choosing to reward your employees and this type of reward has far-reaching benefits. While hiring externally may reduce training time, an internal promotion improves organizational memory. The new recruit may have some technical challenges, but they are already familiar with the staff and their functions. They understand the company, its corporate objectives, the department, its function, and the personnel; these are all things of great value that are not

When you choose to promote from within, you are choosing to reward your employees, and this type of reward has far-reaching benefits.

easily teachable, and only come with time spent within the organization. An internal promotion sends the message to the rest of the organization that hard work will be recognized and rewarded. Add to that an employee referral program and you have dramatically reduced the costs associated with recruiting top-notch employees.

Recruiting internally for open positions is about using the right type of employee in the right position. This means making a commitment to develop your current human capital. Most importantly, it means making recruiting and hiring decisions that consider the "promotability" factor of the candidates.

COMPLETE SELECTION PROCESS

Depending on the level of formality in your organization, you may decide to have a fully documented selection process in place. The selection process includes everything we have discussed and systemizes the information such that all hires are handled in the same way. If your company tends to do a lot of hiring due to seasonal fluctuations, workload variations, high-turnover industry, etc., then the time spent putting together a formal process is very well-spent. The process is fully detailed from the beginning, so there are no unnecessary delays when it comes time to fill positions, it is easy to initiate a hiring because the system is already in place, employees within the company know what to expect when making referrals or being considered for promotion, and the system is fully defensible in the case of legal challenges. The following is an example of a complete selection process model and can be modified to suit your specific needs.

SELECTION-PROCESS GUIDE

A. Position Preview Guide has been prepared for our entry-level Operator position and other positions that we generally hire externally. These Guides provide information about the company, give a brief description of the duties, summarize key employment conditions, and give information about the selection process.

This Guide encourages applicants to "self-select" themselves, and if, after reading the Guide, they are still interested in working at NAYA, there is an application form with instructions included.

B. All applicants are required to submit a formal application. The minimum educational requirement is Grade 12 or equivalent; however, work experience may be considered as an equivalency. Other qualifications include:

- Previous work experience (manufacturing experience is an asset).

- Willing to work flexible hours and shift work including nights and weekends.

- Good interpersonal skills.

- Self-motivated.

- Able to handle multiple tasks.

C.   Applicants who are selected to continue in the selection process will undergo aptitude testing using the General Aptitude Test Battery (GATB), an internationally recognized, standardized employment aptitude test. Some positions may require Mechanical Aptitude testing as well.

D.   Applicants whose aptitude test scores meet or exceed the profile summary for the position they are applying for will be given further consideration through the interview process.

E.   The interview will be behaviorally oriented with questions designed to get detailed, specific information about the applicants' behavior in their previous positions.

F.   Finally, references are checked and an employment decision is made.

G.   There is a formal Orientation and Training program for all new employees.

POSITION PREVIEW GUIDE

Mission Statement:

Insert yours here

History:

Provide a brief corporate history

JOB DESCRIPTION
Bottling Technician Level 1—Millwright Trainee

DIRECT SUPERVISOR: Production/Warehouse Manager

INDIRECT SUPERVISOR: Lead Hand

JOB PURPOSE: Produces Finished Product and Helps Maintain Production-Line Equipment by operating production-line equipment and learning how to repair equipment as directed.

DETAILED DESCRIPTION:
- **Contributes to Production** by observing machine operation, detecting malfunctions, adjusting settings, keeping a tidy work area.

- **Contributes to Continuous Operations** by learning to maintain the production line under a designate's guidance when necessary, learning to perform preventative maintenance as directed, doing minor maintenance as directed.

- **Ensures Quality Product** by following all Company operating procedures, sanitation procedures, other policies and procedures and reporting needed changes.

- **Provides Information** by completing PTP reports, communicating with coworkers interdepartmentally and inter-shift.

- **Maintains a Safe and Healthy Work Environment** by helping to ensure all production equipment is functioning safely, keeping the maintenance shop and other work areas clean, following all Company policies and procedures and following organization standards and legal regulations.

- **Maintains Technical Knowledge** by attending training sessions and reviewing literature/publications.

- **Contributes to the Team Environment** by performing other duties as required.

OPPORTUNITIES AND CHALLENGES

(Company Name) offers a team-oriented work environment with a variety of tasks to be accomplished on every shift. The goal of the management and staff is to have many of the manufacturing functions cross-trained and able to assist wherever necessary to ensure efficient and cost-effective operations in a stimulating work atmosphere.

(Company Name) is committed to staff development through a comprehensive internal training system that covers all the operating equipment and various positions. Certificate training in areas such as WHMIS, Food Safe, Lift Truck, First Aid and Propane Handling will be offered as operational need arises.

(Company Name) is an equal opportunity employer and compensation will be competitive both within the industry and the community.

The Plant is located (miles) east of (city), and employees are responsible for getting themselves to and from work.

The Plant operates 24 hours a day, 7 days a week in high season. Low season scheduling is usually 24 hours a day for 7 days every 2 weeks.

Employees must be willing to work days, nights and weekends to accommodate the production schedule. Most employees work 12-hour shifts, alternating 3 shifts one week and 4 shifts the next.

The industry is subject to seasonal and market fluctuations, and

OPPORTUNITIES AND CHALLENGES (CONTINUED)

employees are laid off by job classification according to company seniority. This means that until sufficient seniority is accumulated, production employees are periodically affected by lay-off due to work shortages.

SELECTION PROCESS

A.   All applicants are required to submit a formal application. The minimum educational requirement is Grade 12 or equivalent; however, work experience may be considered as an equivalency. Other qualifications include:

- Previous work experience (manufacturing experience is an asset).

- Willing to work flexible hours and shift work including nights and weekends.

- Good interpersonal skills.

- Self-motivated.

- Able to handle multiple tasks.

B.   Applicants who are selected to continue in the selection process will undergo aptitude testing using the General Aptitude Test Battery (GATB), an internationally recognized, standardized employment aptitude test. As well, a Mechanical Aptitude test will be administered.

C.   Applicants whose GATB scores meet or exceed the profile summary for "Industrial Mechanics" and who score 75% or better on the Mechanical Aptitude test will be given further consideration through the interview process.

D.   The interview will be behaviorally oriented with questions designed to get detailed, specific information about the applicant's behavior in their previous positions.

Examples:
Flexibility is important in this work environment. Please tell me about a time when you were most flexible in your job.

- When?

- Situation—What was the circumstance?

- Action—What happened? Who else was involved?

- Outcome—What was the outcome?

- Reference—Did anyone comment on your efforts?

In our organization we expect employees to work cooperatively as team members. Please tell me about your best example of working cooperatively as a team member to accomplish an important goal.

- When?

- Situation—What was the goal or objective?

- Action—What was your role?

- Outcome—How did you interact with the other team members?

- Reference—Did anyone comment on your input?

E.   Finally, references are checked and an employment decision is made.

If you are still interested in employment at (Company Name), please fill out the attached Application and include a résumé if desired.

Mail your completed application to:

"Name"
(Company Name)
PO Box xxxx
City, State, Zip

OR

Drop your completed application at the Plant:

Physical Address

Please note: Only applications that are filled out completely will be considered.

EMPLOYMENT APPLICATION

Company Name: _____

Address: _____

City: _____ State: _____ Zip: _____

Phone Number: _____

PERSONAL INFORMATION	
Last Name:	First Name:
Address:	
City:	State:	Zip Code:
Telephone (Home):	(Office):

DESIRED POSITION
Position Requested:
❑ Full-time ❑ Part-time ❑ Seasonal ❑ Day Shift ❑ Evening Shift ❑ Night Shift
Have you ever been employed by our company? If so, when?

EDUCATION			
Level	Date (Month/Year)	Grade/Years Completed	Diploma/ Degree
High School:			
Name:	Starting:	9 10 11 12	Yes No
	Ending:		
College/University			
Name:	Starting:		Yes No
Specialization:	Ending:		
Other Applicable Training			
Name:	Starting:		Yes No
Specialization:	Ending:		

EMPLOYMENT EXPERIENCE	
Company:	Type of enterprise:
Address:	Telephone:
Position:	Name of immediate supervisor:
Length of employment: Start: _____ End: _____ Salary: Start: ___ End: _____	
Reason for departure:	
Description of your tasks:	

Company:	Type of enterprise:
Address:	Telephone:
Position:	Name of immediate supervisor:
Length of employment: Start: _____ End: _____ Salary: Start: ___ End: _____	
Reason for departure:	
Description of your tasks:	

Company:	Type of enterprise:
Address:	Telephone:
Position:	Name of immediate supervisor:
Length of employment: Start: _____ End: _____ Salary: Start: ___ End: _____	
Reason for departure:	
Description of your tasks:	

WORK BEHAVIOR

In this section you are required to answer two behavioral-based questions. These questions are designed to get you to recall a specific event or accomplishment from your past. Be very specific and describe the incident accurately. If you can, include a reference. These references may be contacted so be sure it is someone who witnessed the incident or who can comment on your involvement in the situation. Use the following example to help you answer the two behavior questions:

Example: Organization "A" is committed to exceeding our customers' expectations. Please tell me about a time when you exceeded a customer's expectations.

When:	3 months ago
Situation:	During my shift at the supermarket deli, I was approached by a man who wanted to buy some cold-cuts for an event he was hosting for 50 people. He did not know what kind of meat to buy or how much.
Action:	After talking to him at length, I learned the "event" was a midnight snack at his daughter's wedding. I then helped him choose which meats, suggested how much per person, and suggested attractive ways to make up the trays. He mentioned that in all the confusion he forgot the name of the contact person at the hotel who was looking after the wedding. I asked him which hotel and it turns out a friend of mine worked there so I called and got the name right then and there.
Outcome:	The man left the store feeling much more relaxed and in control of things. He returned a few days after the wedding to thank me for everything and said he got many compliments on the way the trays were arranged.
Frequency:	I am able to help customers like this about once a month.
Reference:	Customer commented to the Store Manager, Mrs. Blackstone, so you can call her at (250) 555-1111.

WORK BEHAVIOR—Question #1	
Flexibility is important in this work environment. Please tell me about a time when you were most flexible in your job. Be very specific and describe one actual incident.	
When:	
Situation: Describe the circumstance in detail.	
Action: Tell me what you did (be specific).	
Outcome: What was the end result?	
Frequency: How often do you do this?	
Reference: Who else was there? Did anyone comment?	

WORK BEHAVIOR—Question #2	
In our organization we expect employees to work cooperatively as team members. Please tell me about your best example of working cooperatively as a team member to accomplish an important goal.	
When:	
Situation: Describe the circumstance in detail.	
Action: Tell me what you did (be specific).	
Outcome: What was the end result?	
Frequency: How often do you do this?	
Reference: Who else was there? Did anyone comment?	

REFERENCES			

Please list the name and contact of three references, excluding blood relations and/or personal friends, that can supply us with professional references concerning your work habits. These can be the same as those included with your answers for the behavior questions:

Name	Occupation	Company	Telephone
Address			
Name	Occupation	Company	Telephone
Address			
Name	Occupation	Company	Telephone
Address			
Name	Occupation	Company	Telephone
Address			

PLEASE READ CAREFULLY BEFORE SIGNING THIS DOCUMENT

I, the undersigned, do clarify that the information listed above on the present application is true and complete. I understand that any false declaration may result in the refusal of my application or the termination of my employment. I authorize (Company Name) to contact my former employer(s) and others listed here for references.

Signature: _____ Date: _____

APPLICATION REVIEW PROCESS

All applications for (Company Name) are reviewed and acknowledged within one month of receipt. The following standards apply:

Education: Grade 12 or equivalent (minimum). Work experience may be considered as an equivalency. (Company Name) is an equal opportunity employer that encourages a 50/50 male/female ratio.

Reference Check: References must be work-related. No personal references. Summer students will be allowed one personal reference due to lack of work experience.

APPLICATION-HANDLING

Action:
Unsolicited Résumé Received

Response:
Send postcard #1 advising need to complete application

Dear Job Applicant:

Thank you very much for your interest in working for (Company Name). For your application to be processed further, we require a formal application to be filled out and submitted to us.

We are not in a hiring position at this time; however, should you wish to submit a formal application, you can pick one up at our Plant at (address).

Sincerely,
(Company Name) Selection Team

Action:

Unsolicited Application Received

Response:

Send postcard #1A advising will keep on file for 90 days

Dear Job Applicant:

Thank you very much for your interest in working for (Company Name). We are not in a hiring position at this time; however, your application will remain on file for 90 days.

Should a suitable opening become available during that time, we will call and advise you if you have been chosen to continue in our selection process.

Sincerely,
(Company Name) Selection Team

Action:
Solicited Application Received

Response:
Send postcard #2 advising will contact in ten days if interested

---

Dear Job Applicant:

Thank you very much for your interest in working for (Company Name). We are currently reviewing you background to determine if there is a match with our staffing needs at this time.

If your background fits our needs, we will contact you within ten days of the postmark on this card.

Sincerely,
(Company Name) Selection Team

Action:
Application Reviewed and Selected to Continue

Response:
Send letter inviting to proceed with pre-employment testing

Dear Job Applicant:

Our Selection Team has reviewed your qualifications and is pleased to inform you that you have been selected to participate in the aptitude testing portion of our recruitment process.

Your aptitude will be assessed in five different areas: General Learning, Verbal, Numerical, Spatial, and Form Perception. The instrument we will be using is the General Aptitude Test Battery (GATB). This is a fully standardized aptitude test used in employment counseling and selection throughout North America.

I will contact you within seven days and advise you of the testing location and date. I have also enclosed a pamphlet for further information on writing aptitude tests. If you have any questions or concerns, please contact me at (250) 555-1111.

Sincerely,
(Name)

Phone applicant to arrange testing; spend some time on the phone with the applicant and conduct impromptu interview (five minutes) discussing his or her background.

Action:

Reviewed Pre-Employment Testing Results

Response:

Send letter — invite to proceed with interviewing

or

Send letter — thank you for participating, no further interest

---

Dear Job Applicant:

On behalf of our Selection Team, I am pleased to inform you that your aptitude scores met or exceeded the minimum standards required for the position of _____ at (Company Name).

We would like to invite you to participate in the next step of our selection process. We will be conducting behavioral-based interviews with questions similar to those you answered on your initial application.

I will call you within seven days to set up an interview time during the week of _____. Congratulations on your fine test results! I look forward to speaking with you soon.

Sincerely,
(Name)

Dear Job Applicant:

Thank you for your participation in our selection process.

On behalf of our Selection Team, I regret to inform you that your aptitude scores did not meet the minimum requirements for the position of _____ at (Company Name).

We thank you for your interest in (Company Name) and wish you success in your future endeavors.

Sincerely,
(Name)

Action
Interview and Reference Check

Response
Phone and make job offer

Send terms and conditions of employment for signature

or

Advise applicant is unsuccessful

Dear Job Applicant:

This letter is to confirm the terms and conditions of your employment with (Company Name).

Date of Hire:

Position:

Wage:

Probationary period:

Union/Non-union:

Benefit eligibility:

Vacation entitlement:

For all other terms and conditions, please refer to the (Company Name) Handbook or Collective Agreement.

Please sign this offer and return to (Name) if you are in agreement.
I HEREBY AGREE TO THE TERMS AND CONDITIONS OF MY EMPLOYMENT WITH (Company Name) AS OUTLINED ABOVE.

Name:_____   Date:_____

Sincerely,
(Name)

Treat the selection process as an extension of your business strategy—look for ways to continuously improve, select people to grow with your company and maximize your people return.

*One of the most profound ways to keep an employee
satisfied and committed to doing a good job is to
communicate effectively with him or her.*

CHAPTER 3

EFFECTIVE COMMUNICATION
Giving and Receiving Information Effectively

*"The art of communication is the
language of leadership."*

—James Humes

Now that you have the right person in the right job, the hard part is over, right? Wrong!

The real work has just begun because now you want to keep that person and not let your competition nab him or her up after you've invested time and money in recruitment and training.

Now that you have hired the person you are sure is right for the job, you must work to keep that employee. One of the most profound ways to keep an employee satisfied and committed to doing a good job is to communicate effectively with him or her. Communication is not simply important, it is the cornerstone of human civilization. Almost everything we do involves or is dependant upon communication. We communicate to learn and to teach, to socialize with others, to entertain and to persuade. We cannot engage in any aspect of business, science, art, finance or engineering without exchanging ideas and information with others — the essence of communication.

Each year, business, industrial and governmental organizations spend billions of dollars trying to communicate with employees, customers, suppliers and with each other. Yet, for all its importance, communication is something that most of us do very poorly. Based on analyses of responses from hundreds of thousands of employees who have responded to employee attitude surveys, the single most common complaint that employees have about their work environment is poor communication — despite the billions of dollars that is spent each year on organizational communication.

Eighty percent of a manager's time is spent in verbal communication.

At least 80 percent of a manager's waking hours are spent in verbal communication, so it is not surprising that interpersonal communication is a hot management topic. In survey after survey, the ability to communicate effectively is ranked as the number-one management skill and the key factor contributing to organizational problems. All agree that more communication is better than less, but it still remains a major source of discord between management and employees. Why does this problem persist?

The main reason is that most people think of themselves as effective communicators and blame everyone else for communication breakdown. So while most people agree that proficient interpersonal communication is critical to a business's success, most individuals don't feel a strong need to improve their own skill level.

So even if you think you're an effective communicator, read the next section; there is always the possibility you will glean one gem of information.

COMMUNICATION BASICS

Exactly what is communication and how does it work? Most of us think of communication as talking to someone else. Or, maybe writing somebody a letter or sending them an e-mail message. That's part of it, of course, but in reality, communication is a very complicated process.

The Communication Process

In order for communication as we know it to exist, there must be a minimum of three elements:

1. Message

Basically, this is a thought. The thought, or message, must be put into a form that can be sent to someone. The form can be oral, written, digital, pictorial, graphic or some other form that will be understood by another person.

2. Sender

This is the person who has the thought or message to be sent to someone else.

3. Receiver

This is the person who gets the message that is sent by the receiver.

The sender has a message that he or she wants to send to someone else—the receiver. The first challenge is that the sender must take the thought, which is the basis of the message, and encode it or put it into a form in which it can be transmitted to the receiver. The sender immediately encounters all kinds of problems as he or she begins this process. For example, there may be language and semantic problems. The sender must make sure that the message is accurate, that what is communicated is what the sender meant to say. The message must be directed to the correct audience or receiver, and methods of transmitting the message must be selected.

The process is no easier for the receiver. There are many barriers through which the message must pass before it reaches the receiver. The receiver must decode the message through his or her own screen of barriers, like preconceptions, prejudice, culture, personality, distractions, and a lot more, before communication can be completed. Then, in order to close the communication loop, the receiver must respond to the message in some way. This usually involves the receiver becoming a sender of a return message, like feedback, and the process repeats itself in reverse.

> *"You can have brilliant ideas, but if you*
> *can't get them across, your ideas*
> *won't get you anywhere."*
>
> —Lee Iacocca

Communication Channels

An important part of the communication process is the decision as to whether the message should be in written or verbal form; how it should be sent through which particular channels. Should the message, for example, be posted on the company bulletin board, be conveyed through the mail, sent via computer modem, or be delivered in person? Would a picture or graphics help the receiver understand the message better? The message could also be sent via television, radio, two-way transceivers, or announced over the loudspeaker.

Whew! No wonder things get messed up when we try to explain something to another person or when a boss tries to give clear work instructions to an employee. Clear, precise, understandable communication is really very difficult to achieve, but the good news is that it is not impossible to accomplish; the first step in effective communication is effective listening.

Active Listening

"Listening is the single skill that makes the difference between a mediocre and a great company."

–Lee Iacocca

Listening is one of the most important skills that you can have. How well you listen has a major impact on your job effectiveness and on the quality of your personal life. Our listening effectiveness directly affects our ability to respond to what we hear in an accurate, appropriate and timely manner. But, here is the problem: It has been clinically proven that the listening effectiveness of the average person, before training in listening skills, is only 25

*How well you listen has a major impact on your job effective-
ness and on the quality of your personal life. The average
person really listens effectively only 25 percent of the time.*

percent. This means that when the average person finishes
having a 10-minute conversation with someone, like a boss,
customer, friend or neighbor, he or she has understood and
can respond accurately and appropriately to only 2.5 minutes
worth of what was said. Imagine if the productivity of the
average worker was that low!

Failure to listen effectively to others is one of the leading
causes of misunderstanding and conflict. Poor listening skills
result in more job-related interpersonal problems than any
other cause. The failure to listen to customers effectively

results in more lost business, late deliveries and most other service quality deficiencies than poor product quality. Failure to listen effectively is perhaps the single leading cause of employee dissatisfaction in the workplace.

Active listening is the term that has been given to the one of the best ways to become a more effective listener. To be an active listener, you must hear the words and understand the total message. This means you must make a conscious effort to hear not only the words that another person is saying, but, more importantly, to try to understand the total message being sent by the other person. In order to do this you must pay attention to the other person very carefully. You cannot allow yourself to become distracted by what else may be going on in the room or area where the conversation is being held. Nor can you allow yourself to become distracted by disinterest in what the other person is saying or by trying to form counter arguments that you will launch as soon as the other person stops speaking. All of these barriers, and more like them, are exactly why the average person really listens effectively only 25 percent of the time.

Have you ever been engaged in a conversation when you wondered if the other person truly understands or cares what you are saying? Have you ever been unsure if your message was getting across or if it was really worthwhile to continue to speak? The chances are that more than once you found yourself speaking to someone who was totally non-responsive. It probably was like you were talking to a stone wall. If so, then you experienced exactly the opposite of active listening on the part of your communication partner. Active listening also means acknowledging that you hear and are listening to what is being said—even if you do not agree with it. A nod of the listener's head does not necessarily mean agreement. Don't be afraid to use body language gestures and other signs to acknowledge that you are listening to the other person. Finally, you need to encourage the person to keep speaking. While you indicate to the other person that you are paying attention to what they are saying, you must respond in a way that will both encourage the other person to keep speaking until they have conveyed their whole message. This means asking for clarification or recapping what was said as well as directly asking for more information.

To be an active listener, you must:

- Pay attention to the speaker: look at him or her directly, put aside distracting thoughts, pay close attention to the speaker's body language, do not engage in side conversations while the person is speaking.

- Show that you hear what the person is saying: nod your head or make other indications of acknowledgment.

- Encourage the speaker to provide you with more information: recapping in your own words what you believe the speaker to have said and meant, ask for clarification or additional information.

- Defer judgment: wait until the speaker presents his or her opinions before expressing your own, don't interrupt with counter arguments midway in a sentence.

- Respond appropriately: be candid, open and honest in your response.

By learning and focusing on the communication basics, we will improve the accuracy of the message. This is the first step in effective communication, but effective interpersonal communication goes beyond accuracy and delves into meanings and interpretations. Even if you communicate accurately, people still become offended with one another, they still make insulting comments, and they still communicate clumsily. Who says what to whom, what is said, why it is said and how it is said all have an effect on the relationships between people. When people communicate using brash, insensitive and unproductive comments, it is the interpersonal aspect of the communication that hampers delivery rather than the accuracy. Ineffective communication leads people to dislike each other, lose confidence in each other, refuse to listen to each other and generally disrespect each other.

Communication is as much a matter of human relationships as it is about transmitting facts.

Ultimately, a poor manager/employee relationship is what leads people to look for new jobs. So how do you stop the cycle? It's called supportive communication—where mangers communicate accurately and honestly without jeopardizing the interpersonal relationship.

SUPPORTIVE COMMUNICATION

In supportive communication, the relationship between the two parties is supported, even enhanced, by the interchange. This does not mean promoting likability or social acceptance over honesty and candor; it simply means delivering the message in a way that is sensitive to the other person's thoughts and feelings. Positive interpersonal relationships have practical and instrumental value to organizations; those organizations enjoy higher productivity, faster problem-solving, higher-quality output and fewer conflicts and counterproductive behavior. It is very relevant and in a company's best interest to have managers use

Supportive communicators deliver their message in a way that is sensitive to the other person's thoughts and feelings.

supportive communication and help all employees to use this type of communication in the workplace.

The most obvious times to use and practice supportive communication is when a manger finds themselves having to coach or counsel an employee. Whenever a person is faced with constructive criticism, it is a very difficult time. The first barrier to communication is defensiveness. When one individual feels threatened or punished by the communication, they tend to protect themselves; focusing more on self-preservation than on listening. The second barrier that gets put up is disconfirmation. This happens when one party feels put-down or insignificant because of the communication. Their focus is then on bolstering themselves rather than listening. In order to overcome these barriers, it is important to practice supportive communication.

Principles of Supportive Communication
Supportive communication is problem-oriented, not person-oriented.
Problem-oriented communication focuses on problems and solutions rather than on personal traits. Person-oriented focuses on an individual's characteristics or motives and not an event. When a comment focuses on the situation at hand, it is more relevant and the person can detach themselves and their self-worth from the comment. This is important when giving praise as well as criticism; praising a person is not motivating ("You're great.") but praising what they did is ("You facilitated that meeting superbly.").

Person-Oriented Comments vs. Problem-Oriented Comments	
Person-Oriented Comments	**Problem-Oriented Comments**
"You're really hard to work with."	"I have held three meetings this week and you haven't attended any of them."
"Great job! You're terrific!"	"The detail you put into that report was excellent; it really helped sell the project to the investors."
"You have to be more understanding."	"Bob is having a tough time with his divorce, I think we should ask him what we can do to help."

Effective supportive communicators don't have to avoid expressing personal opinions or feelings, but they need to make sure the comments are nonjudgmental.

Supportive communication is based on congruence, not incongruence.

Congruent communication matches what is being said verbally or nonverbally, to what is being felt or thought. Incongruence at work most often occurs when there is a mismatch between what a person feels and what they actually communicate. Usually a person who is angry at something will deny it to avoid a confrontation. Genuine, honest statements are always better than artificial or dishonest ones, but that does not mean it is okay to just spout off about everything and anything because it is truly how you feel.

| Non-Congruent Comments vs. Congruent Comments ||
Non-Congruent Comments	Congruent Comments
"Do I seem upset? No, everything is fine."	"Your behavior really upset me."
"Oh, don't worry about it; it's fine."	"I felt so insignificant when you forgot to introduce me."
"Feedback on the production plan? Uh, the boss liked it."	"You know that production plan you drew up? The boss asked me to fix a few things. Come here and I'll show what to be careful of for next time."

It is important to keep in mind that supportive communication is honest, but it does not offend.

Supportive communication is descriptive, not evaluative.
When communicating a problem, it is hard not to slip into judgment or labeling. The evaluation leaves the person feeling under attack and they are likely to respond defensively. When you use descriptive words to communicate a problem, you explain it objectively and from your own point of view, and you always make a suggestion for improvement. There is no focus of good or bad, right or wrong; the conversation simply focuses on what happened, how it affected you, and how it should be handled in the future.

Evaluative Comments vs. Descriptive Comments	
Evaluative Comment	**Descriptive Comment**
"You performed abysmally last month!"	"You finished fewer projects last month than any other associate. I'm concerned about our productivity levels. Let's meet weekly to keep on track and help you complete three more projects this month."

By describing the event and the consequences and suggesting a way to improve, you are fostering trust, and the person does not feel attacked or maligned. Most often they will agree to work with you to improve and appreciate the honest and forthright approach.

Supportive communication validates rather than invalidates the person.

When a person acts superior, rigid or indifferent when communicating a message, they are invalidating the other person and setting up the conversation for failure. Invalidating behaviors include not letting the other finish a sentence, telling the person their ideas are not worthy or ill-informed, being a know-it-all, using words or jargon the other person can't understand, or acting indifferently with silence or unrelated activity. When a person feels invalidated, it is more destructive than harsh criticism or disagreement; the person is left feeling unworthy and unredeemable. When you validate someone in a conversation, that means you treat him or her as an equal, you are flexible, you have a two-way dialogue, and you try to reach mutual agreement.

Invalidating Comments vs. Validating Comments	
Invalidating Comments	**Validating Comments**
"You don't understand the project well enough, so we'll just do it my way."	"I know I have a few ideas to improve the process but I was wondering what your thoughts were."
"You really shouldn't feel that way."	"I guess my remark was too brash, and I can see that I've hurt your feelings. Can we grab a coffee and talk about it to clear the air?"

Validating people creates feelings of self-worth and self-confidence that translate into self-motivation and improved performance.

Supportive communication is specific not general.

The more specific a statement is, the more useful it is in terms of improvement. Telling someone he or she is poor at managing time is less useful than telling him or her that the hour they spent scheduling meetings could have been done by their assistant. Specific statements avoid extremes and absolutes (never, always, completely) and use qualifiers instead (generally, frequently, appears to be).

General Comments vs. Specific Comments	
General Comments	**Specific Comments**
"You're always interrupting me!"	"You interrupted me three times in that meeting."
"You have no consideration for others' feelings."	"When you reacted sarcastically to my request, you gave me the impression you don't care about how I feel."
"You never ask for my advice."	"You made the decision yesterday to book our annual convention without asking my advice, but I'm a keynote speaker for a conference that week. Let's get together and work out a time and place that accommodates everyone."

Specific communication is useful to the extent that it focuses on an identifiable problem or behavior about which something can be done.

Supportive communication is owned not disowned.

When you take responsibility for your comments, you own the communication. Words that indicate ownership include "I," "me" and "mine." When you talk in third person or first person-plural, "we think," they said" or "one might say," you disown the message by attributing it to an external source. When conversation is not owned, the receiver never knows whose point of view is being expressed and is apt to misinterpret it. When you own communication, you indicate a willingness to invest in the relationship and work toward a solution.

General Comments vs. Specific Comments	
Disowned Comments	**Owned Comments**
"It's a great idea, but they just won't approve it."	"I've decided to nix your project suggestion for now."
"Everyone says you're unhappy; you gotta cheer up."	"It is my understanding that you are feeling unappreciated. Can we talk about it?"
"It seems our bonuses are getting cut this year."	"I have to tell you that our profits are down so the bonus program is being scaled back this year."

Owned communication gives the receiver confidence in the legitimacy of the message and in the intention of the message conveyor.

Supportive communication requires listening, not one-way message delivery.

This is active listening, where you respond appropriately to the other person's message. In any conversation, the person who talks the most learns the least about the other person; good supervision requires good listening. Good listening means you advise, provide direction, deflect comments, probe for more information, and reflect back or mirror the comments to ensure full understanding.

General Comments vs. Specific Comments	
One-Way Message Delivery	**Supportive Listening**
"I told you to stack the boxes five high."	"I know you're concerned that the boxes will tip; we've checked with the manufacturer and they are rated to stack six high, so at five we should be safe."
"I'm sick and tired of your excuses. Don't be late again!"	"I know you're having a tough time balancing work and school, but being late is just not acceptable."

Supportive, or active, listening requires slowing down and allowing the other person to be as much a part of the conversation as you are.

QUICK GUIDE TO INTERPERSONAL COMMUNICATION

Supportive communication is the best and most holistic way to improve your interpersonal skills. The quick and easy way is to remember and use these three suggestions the next time you experience a somewhat difficult interpersonal relationship situation.

Know Yourself

Improvement must begin from within yourself. You are at the same time your greatest strength and your worst enemy. The more that you know about your own feelings, emotions, emotional control, ambitions, goals, sensitivities, personal traits, attributes, skills and deficiencies, the better you will be able to respond to interpersonal communication situations effectively. Everything that you communicate to another person is a function of all of these. If you combine the quality of knowing yourself with the practice of thinking before you speak, you will be better able to ensure that what you say to someone else is positive, constructive and helpful rather than offensive or insensitive.

Develop Empathy

A simple definition of empathy is put yourself in the other person's shoes. How do you want someone else to communicate with you? If you are a clerk in a store, how do you feel when an insensitive customer berates you for a store policy that he or she does not like? You didn't make

When communicating with someone, look for signs of apprehension, hope, bewilderment, agreement, lack of agreement, or any other emotion.

the policy and you probably are not being paid enough to take all of the verbal abuse that the customer is throwing at you, right? Well then, don't speak to someone else like that yourself. When you are communicating with someone else, look for signs that might signal conditions like apprehension, nervousness, hope, anticipation, bewilderment, agreement, lack of agreement or any other emotion or state of mind that could affect how the other person receives and interprets your message. Then imagine yourself in the situation that you are observing and think about how you can shape your communication so that it is appropriate for those particular circumstances. You will avoid making a lot of communication mistakes if you use this simple technique.

Drop the Negatives

Years ago there was a popular motivational technique called positive reinforcement. The idea was that people would respond best to performance counseling if the boss always coached them in positive terms. For example, suppose that the production quota for a worker was 50 widgets per hour but the worker was only doing 40. At the same time, the worker was faithfully and accurately filling out his hourly production rate card by marking that he made 40 widgets per hour. Instead of the boss telling the worker that he was 10 widgets per hour short, he would look for something positive to say and the scenario would sound something like this:

> "Tom, I want to talk to you about your production rate. I have noticed that every hour you make an accurate record of the number of widgets that you produce, which is 40. Thank you for being consistently accurate in your recordkeeping. The quota for widget production, of course, is 50 per hour. Now, how can I help you move from 40 per hour to 50?"

A lot of studies showed that positive reinforcement worked pretty well and many companies paid a great deal of money training their supervisors in that technique. Unfortunately, motivational techniques come and go fairly quickly in industry, so you don't hear much about positive reinforcement anymore. But it does work and it has definite application to just about any form of interpersonal communication. In order to use it, simply focus on the positive while at the same time maintaining honesty and candor. You will find that people respond much better to you and to what you are saying if you give them a little credit at the same time.

Interpersonal communication has such a significant impact on the quality of our work lives, and the most pervasive barriers to effective communication in organizations stem from interpersonal issues. The other major source of communication breakdown is due to the information gap, or the lag between what management knows and when they know it compared to the rest of the organization.

Team Communication
What Teamwork Is All About

Most people would agree that it is important for each of us to be a productive, competent individual contributor whether at work or off the job. The concept of "a fair day's pay for a fair day's work" is based on the premise that each of us will use our skills and talents to the best of our ability in whatever task we are assigned. The same holds true in an off-the-job environment like when we are doing volunteer work for a local charity or for our religious organization or when we are participating as members of a fraternal or social organization.

But in today's highly competitive world, life is getting tougher for the "loner." It is no longer sufficient just to be a good, solid individual contributor. In order to be successful in our modern world, one must also practice effective teamwork.

The term "teamwork" has become very common in both our personal and business lives. Unfortunately, it may suffer from over-usage and misusage. A lot of people talk about teamwork, being a team player or being part of a team. Not everyone who uses those terms, though, understands what teamwork really is or how it works. For example, some people think that simply being part of a group means that they are part of a team. But, groups are not necessarily teams. In fact, there can be a very considerable difference between a team and a group, even though groups and teams may share some of the same characteristics. People in teams, for example, share a common purpose, common attitudes and a sense of unity. People in a group do not necessarily share those characteristics with each other. In addition, in order for a group to be a team there must be something more.

Groups are not necessarily teams. There can be a very considerable difference between a team and a group. People in teams, share a common purpose, common attitudes and a sense of unity.

Members of a team are also mutually committed to achieve a common goal. They fully share information that is relevant about their task or mission with each other in an open, honest and candid way. All of the members of a team actively participate in the team's problem-solving efforts to the full limit of their individual and collective capabilities. Team members encourage each other and try to tap the full creative potential of all team members. They have a special sense of team loyalty and cohesiveness. When disagreement or conflict arises, they deal with it openly and constructively using problem-solving rather than suppression or compromise. Further, team members share responsibility as well as rewards or recognition for their accomplishments.

On the surface you might think that the description also fits practically any group, but this is not the case. For example, a group is still a group if there is unresolved conflict among group members or if some group members withhold relevant problem-solving information from the others. If this occurs, the group is most definitely not a team. The importance of this difference is that teams are capable of doing something that is impossible for most groups. While it is true that the product of a group can be superior to the product of the average individuals within the group, it usually takes a team to achieve synergism.

Synergism occurs when the product of the team is superior to the product of the best, not average, individual on the team. In other words, in teams two plus two can equal more than four! This is why effective teamwork is so important to your company's success. The modern business or social organization is built on the concept of teamwork — everyone within the organization, at all organizational levels, working collaboratively toward a common goal. Individual contributors, no matter how competent in their personal skill area, will simply not be as successful in these types of organizations unless they also know how to effectively communicate and interact with other members of their work or social team.

Team Communication

The kind of information that teams and individual team members may have is almost limitless. Information that is relevant to a team's mission in a business organization may concern production schedules, customer complaints, engineering design studies, product inventories, sales records or budget data. In a hospital, information needed by a team could range from patient admission data, pharmaceutical supplies and laboratory procedures to the condition of the physical facilities, nurse training courses and community-relations programs. In all cases, individual team members have certain pieces of the needed information that can and must be shared fully, openly and candidly with other team members, and the team must know how to access the information they need that none of them possess.

Once a team gathers and shares the required information, they must process or use it to solve a problem or make a decision.

Once a team gathers and shares the required information, they must process or use it to solve a problem or make a decision. In order to do this, teams must have two crucial sets of skills: interaction skills and task function skills. Interaction skills are those skills which maintain good, harmonious relations among team members, resolve any conflict or disagreement that may arise, and encourage full participation and involvement by all team members in the team's task. Task function skills relate mainly to the method by which the team deals with the information it has available; in other words, the extent to which the team uses both rational (scientific) and creative decision-making/problem-solving methods and techniques.

Becoming a Better Team Communicator
Training in team skills is important for all employees. Here are the basics:

- **Think teamwork.** Think in terms of cooperating and collaborating with others. Maintain your skills and competencies as an individual contributor. But at the same time, think about how being an active, effective team participant can benefit you and about what you can do, as a team member, to help and benefit others.

- **Share information.** This may not be easy, especially for strong, competent individual contributors who are accustomed to making decisions alone. It is true that information is power, but the real power comes from sharing information, from being an open source of information that helps to empower others. Don't forget: sharing information also means sharing your ideas and suggestions.

- Be an open communicator. Open, honest, candid communication — information sharing — is a requisite of effective team communication.

- **Practice inclusion.** This means involving others in the decision-making and problem-solving process. Passive, one-way communication, no matter how open, will not optimize team communication. Some people are quieter than others, but that does not mean that they do not want to communicate or that they do not want to share information; they may only need encouragement. Actively involve other team members in the team discussion. Ask for their input and phrase your questions so that they cannot be answered by a simple yes or no.

- **Know the subject.** Subject knowledge will increase your problem-solving competencies. People naturally feel more confident and comfortable about speaking up when they can do so from a solid knowledge base.

- **Follow a rational process.** Don't shoot from the hip and try to solve the problem before you have even defined the problem issue. This is often what happens when people do not follow a rational problem-solving and decision-making process. If you are not familiar with this process, just follow these six easy steps the next time that you are confronted with a team problem:

  1. Define the specific problem issue.
  2. Gather all of the relevant facts.
  3. Review and analyze the facts.

4. Develop decision alternatives.
5. Evaluate the decision alternatives.
6. Decide and act.

- **Be creative.** Being creative or innovative is not in conflict with the rational problem-solving process. There are rules and procedures for even the most open-ended creative techniques like brainstorming. The basic concept of creative problem-solving is "deferred judgment." This means that at the beginning of the process there is a lot of brainstorming, the generation of many creative ideas. The evaluation of those ideas follows later.

- **Review and critique.** Continuous improvement should be important to all teams. Because communication is such an integral part of team interaction, good team communicators frequently conduct a self-critique to ensure that they are following constructive communication practices. In fact, the entire team should periodically pause and

Successful teamwork relies on effective communication, and teams are critical to a company's success.

ask themselves how well they are communicating with each other; that is, how well they are sharing and processing information. They should tackle any communication barriers they might find just like they would any other problem.

Being part of a team can be a fun and rewarding experience. Participating with others in decision-making and problem-solving activities leads to better quality results without sacrificing one's own skills and attributes as a competent individual contributor. The learning experience of being involved in team activities also is an excellent way to achieve growth in one's job or career. Successful teamwork is largely a function of effective communication, and teams are critical to a company's success. Learn to be a team player and encourage your employees to be team players; two heads are better than one, and the more heads you have on your side the better!

THE INFORMATION GAP

"They just don't seem to get it."
"Why can't they see what needs to be done?"
"How can they be so out of touch with reality?"

How often have you heard these remarks in the hallways, meeting rooms, cafeterias and offices of your organization, and is it management talking about their employees, or employees talking about their managers? This gap in understanding between managers and employees leads to confusion and conflict; breakdown in communication between management and employees impedes the effectiveness, productivity and satisfaction of people. Reducing the understanding gap is critical in maintaining an attractive work environment, but what causes the gap in the first place?

The main reason for the gap is that employees are responsible for the direct production or delivery of goods and services, and management is responsible for presenting the corporate vision while supervising and coordinating the daily work of the employees. This means that mangers see the "big picture" and expect their employees to work toward the "big picture" without necessarily letting them in on what the "big picture" actually looks like. This is not usually done intentionally or with malice, it is just an expeditious way to get things done. The problem is that when employees can't see how their work fits into and contributes to the company's success, they become tunnel-visioned, focusing on their own little sphere rather than the company as a whole. When changes are needed or accommodations requested, the uninformed employee becomes defensive and sometimes angry; charging that the change is only being implemented to hamper their work life.

When employees can't see how their work fits into and contributes to the company's success, they become tunnel-visioned, focusing on their own little sphere rather than the company as a whole.

Employees often have little to no time or are given little information to process and rationalize the changes. This produces a great deal of personal and professional stress, and it contributes significantly to employee dissatisfaction. To fully connect employees with the organization—and diminish the understanding gap—business must include employees in the company's visions and goals and work as a unit to engage everyone in the process.

What Engages Employees?

- When they have an opportunity to provide input in the decision-making process.

- When they can assume responsibility and authority for their own work with the ability to choose how their work is to be done.

- When they work in a collegial manner with managers, each respecting and accepting the roles and responsibilities of the other.

Open Communication

Have you ever experienced less than honest, fully candid communication from a colleague, supervisor or your own employees? Perhaps no one was exactly dishonest with you but instead, information vital to your task or work assignment was intentionally withheld from you.

Information Is Power

A manager in Department A may have information that is essential to the effective operation of Department B, managed by her rival. She intentionally withholds that information, both to make the manager of Department B look bad and also to make herself look better when she uses it to her advantage at a later meeting with her superior. Or, how about situations like when executives of the of XYZ Company know that next month it will be necessary to layoff 10 percent of the workforce—for very valid economic reasons. But, they are afraid that if they give the workforce a month's notice, the better employees will "bail out" and seek employment with the competition. So when the production manager tells senior management about a layoff rumor, they lie to him and he, in turn, assures the workforce that there will be no layoffs. Four weeks later, at 4:30 p.m. on a Friday, 10 percent of the employees receive a layoff notice with their final paychecks.

In order to have a successful business or work relationship with a boss, a fellow worker or a subordinate, there also must exist a high degree of mutual trust and respect. One of the best ways to achieve this is by practicing open communication; by being honest and candid when you say something to the other person or share information

If you are in a work situation and you have information that will help your employees and coworkers, share it openly and fully.

with him or her. Sound, accurate business decisions and the solution to business problems must be based on full, complete and accurate information-sharing. That's what open communication is all about.

Share Information Fully

In the long run, you gain very little by being "close to the chest" with information that is needed by others. If you are in a work situation and you have information that will help your employees and coworkers, then by all means share it openly and fully. Yes, information is power, but there is a mistaken notion that one's power is enhanced by keeping a tight rein on information and releasing it only when it is to your advantage to do so. The truth is that there are several forms of legitimate power and all of them require that information be shared openly, honestly, candidly and fully by the information holder to all who need that information to make decisions, solve problems and to otherwise perform their job responsibilities effectively.

Yes, there are certain risks in practicing open communication. It is always possible that a less honorable rival may use your openness to his or her advantage and to your disadvantage or that the person does not really care to hear what you have to say, but for the sake of productivity and job satisfaction, it is important to find that out sooner rather than later.

COMMON COMMUNICATION PITFALLS

Among the ways that we can improve communication is to understand the most common communication pitfalls so that we can avoid falling into them. Some of the most common and important pitfalls include:

Improperly Formed Messages
You will remember that in the first part of the communication process the communicator must somehow take his or her thought, the message, and translate or encode it into a form that can be sent to and understood by someone else. This becomes a potential communication barrier. The communicator must be very sure that his or her message

has been properly encoded. If not, it will probably be misunderstood. That is why one of the most important stems in achieving good, clear communication is to say what you mean!

Poor Listening Habits

Effective listening is an art and a skill. One of the reasons for this is that the average person's brain is capable of processing information much more rapidly than the rate at which we hear the spoken word. For example, most of us speak at a rate of 160 to 175 words per minute. But our brains can process information at three times that rate. We tend to fill in that extra time by allowing our minds to wander, prematurely evaluating what is being said, developing counter arguments, or by just shutting the other person off mentally.

Misuse of Communication Channels

Far too often we use the wrong method to get our message across to the other person. We write a memo or letter or send an e-mail when we should either pick up the telephone or walk over to the next department to speak directly with the other person. In today's information age, many organizations are beginning to use televised announcements

With the increasing use of technology to convey information, such as e-mail, we are beginning to lose the benefits of two-way communications.

and other electronic one-way mass communication methods to convey messages to many employees rapidly and simultaneously. But in the process, we are beginning to lose the benefits of two-way communication, especially the feedback that comes from employees during post meeting question and answer periods.

Lack of Trust, Credibility and Candor

This is a two-way communication pitfall. People who have information that is important to others and should be communicated to them may not trust the other person (employee, boss, coworker). As a result they withhold vital information (failure to communicate), use it for manipulative purposes, or release only part of the information. We can see this happening ever more frequently today among high-profile public officials. At the same time, justifiably or not, some message receivers, like employees, have developed a deep sense of suspicion and mistrust of communication that comes from the management and supervision of their

Biases, prejudices, likes, dislikes and emotions are all attitude-related attributes that can cloud either message-sending or receiving.

The workplace environment itself can hinder effective communication due to noise or other distractions.

organization. When this happens, another communication pitfalls exists because suspicion, mistrust and perceived lack of message-sender credibility will distort the decoding and interpretation of messages.

Poor Attitude

This covers a series of related communication pitfalls. Often what a person communicates to others and how he or she communicates it is affected by that person's attitude. The issue of trust, credibility and candor is related to attitude. In addition, though, one's biases, prejudices, beliefs, likes, dislikes and emotions are all attitude-related attributes that can cloud either message-sending or receiving. In order to avoid this pitfall, you should try to be as objective as possible when communicating with others. Put aside emotion and any attitude attribute that can distort the clarity, accuracy and completeness of the message that you are sending or of your ability to properly receive the sender's message.

Other communication pitfalls that adversely affect listening include excessive noise and distraction, poor eye contact and insensitive use of body language. Even mechanical or electronic elements are among the many additional barriers to communication that all of us must avoid. Improving communication in the workplace necessarily improves interpersonal relationships, and that is the foundation for a happy, healthy and productive work environment. Humans are social beings and, as such, we need to get along with one another, feel respected and feel appreciated.

Improving communication in the workplace necessarily improves interpersonal relationships, and that is the foundation for a happy, healthy and productive work environment.

CHAPTER 4

TRAINING

Improving Employee Performance

*"Never tell people how to do things.
Tell them what to do and they
will surprise you with their ingenuity."*

—Gen. George S. Patton

What is the best way to ensure you keep that employee you just spent so much time and energy hiring? Orient them to the workplace and help them fit into the organization.

EMPLOYEE ORIENTATION

Orienting employees to their workplaces and their jobs is one of the most neglected functions in many organizations. An employee handbook and piles of paperwork are not sufficient anymore when it comes to welcoming a new employee to your organization. The most frequent complaints about new employee orientation are that it is overwhelming, boring or that the new employee is left to sink or swim. The result is often a confused new employee who is not productive and is more likely to leave the organization within a year.

The orientation program has to be carefully planned to educate the employee about the values, history and who is who in the organization. A well-thought-out orientation program, whether it lasts one day or six months, will help not only in retention of employees, but also in productivity. Organizations that have good orientation programs get new people up to speed faster, have better alignment between what the employees do and what the organization needs them to do, and have lower turnover rates.

Purposes of Orientation
Reduce Startup Costs
Proper orientation can help the employee get "up to speed" much more quickly and reduce the costs associated with learning the job.

Reduce Anxiety
Any new employee, regardless of their vast wealth of experience, feels a certain degree of anxiety when put in a new workplace. Work life is much more than the day-to-day tasks, it's getting to know the people and employees, the office politics, and the "way things are done around here." Proper orientation helps to reduce anxiety that results from entering into an unknown situation and provide guidelines for behavior and conduct so the employee doesn't have to experience the stress of guessing.

Reduce Employee Turnover
Employee turnover increases as employees feel they are not

valued or are put in positions where they don't have the tools necessary to do their jobs. Orientation shows that the organization values the employee and helps provide the tools required for success.

Save Time

The better the initial orientation, the less likely supervisors and coworkers will have to spend time teaching the employee.

Develop Realistic Job Expectations

It is important that employees learn as soon as possible what is expected of them

Proper orientation helps to reduce anxiety that results from entering into an unknown situation, and helps provide guidelines for behavior and conduct.

and what to expect from others, in addition to learning about the values and attitudes of the organization. If you let new employees learn from experience alone they will make many mistakes that are unnecessary and potentially damaging. All new employees should complete a new employment orientation program that is designed to assist them in adjusting to their jobs and work environment and to instill a

Make the new employee feel welcome and part of your organization.

positive work attitude and motivation at the onset.

A thoughtful new employee orientation program can reduce turnover and save an organization thousands of dollars. One reason people change jobs is because they never feel welcome or part of the organization they join. The most important principle to convey during an orientation is your commitment to continuous improvement and continual learning. That way, new employees become comfortable with asking questions to obtain the information they need to learn, problem-solve and make decisions.

A well-thought-out orientation process takes energy, time and commitment, and it usually pays off for the individual employee, the department and the organization.

Tips for New Employee Orientation

Managers and supervisors need to consider key orientation planning questions before implementing or revamping a current program. Important questions to ask are:

- What does the new employee need to know about this work environment to make him or her feel comfortable and confident?

- What impression do you want the new employee to have on his or her first day?

- What policies and procedures are absolutely necessary for new employees to learn and be made aware of on the first day? This vital information must be included in the orientation process.

- What can management do to introduce new employees to their coworkers without having them feel overwhelmed and intimidated?

- What special things (desk, work area, equipment, special instructions) can you provide to make new employees feel comfortable, welcome and secure?

- What can you do to ensure the new employee feels valued by the company at the end of his or her first day?

- How can you ensure that the new employee's supervisor is available to assist him or her on the first day, providing personal care and attention and letting the new employee know that he or she is an important addition to the work team?

Once you've developed a plan that addresses the above questions, you must concentrate on giving the employee a great first impression of your company. This begins as soon as the offer letter of employment is sent; this letter sets the expectations of the job and provides an open avenue of communication before the employee's first day.

Orientation Day

- Make sure the new employee's work area is ready and comfortable.

- Make sure key coworkers know the employee is starting, and encourage them to come to say hello before orientation begins.

- Assign a mentor or partner to show the new person around, make introductions and start training.

- Start with the basics. Don't overwhelm the employee and don't cram everything they need to know into a one-hour session. People become productive sooner if they are firmly grounded in the basic knowledge they need to understand their job. Focus on the why, when, where and how of the position before handing them an assignment or project.

- Provide an orientation packet that includes samples of forms as well as the job description.

- Make the process fun and interesting. Don't simply read through the employee handbook and call it done; hit the highlights of the policy and procedure stuff and use games to aid the learning process. Some game ideas:

- Photo match: After touring the facility, the new employee is given photos of the other employees they just met and a list of names. The object of the game is to match the photos to the names.

- Trivia quiz: Prepare a set of questions (no more than ten) that you have provided answers to during the orientation program. Give out promotional goods or other prizes for completing the quiz.

- Provide a list of frequently asked questions with a contact person/department and phone number or extension.

- Plan to take the new employee to lunch (or join him or her for lunch), and ask the supervisor and available coworkers to join you. There is nothing more uncomfortable than facing a lunchroom of strangers or slinking out for a solitary lunch on your first day.

- Give the new person some responsibility for his or her own orientation. Offer opportunities for self-directed learning, under appropriate supervision.

- Ask for feedback. Find out from former new hires how they perceived the orientation process, and don't be afraid to make changes based on those recommendations.

SAMPLE ORIENTATION OUTLINE
DURATION: 8 hours
MATERIALS: Welcome Package

8:30 a.m.	**The Company and Its Products (0.5)** **Plant Director/Alternate**
	Provide broad overview of (Company)—the company and its products
	History
	Vision/Mission statement
	Marketing slogan
	Corporate philosophy
	View corporate video–H/R
9:00 a.m.	**Department Structure (0.5)** **Supervisor**
	Organization chart with pictures
	Department summary
	Production & Maintenance
	Quality control
	Distribution
	Administration
9:30 a.m.	**Plant Tour (0.5)** **Supervisor**
	Introduce employees as encounter them (at least one per department)

	Visit all departments
	Discuss bottling process/visit all the machines
	Lunchroom
	Time cards
	Exits

10:00 a.m.	**Pop Quiz (for group session only) (0.5)** **Supervisor**
	Questions
	Name product (Company) produces 2 point
	Name two departments 2 points each
	Name two employees they met 5 points each
	What is (Company) marketing slogan? 10 points
	10 or more points gets a business pen

10:30 a.m.	**Break (0.25)**
10:45 a.m.	**Employment Conditions (0.25)** **H/R**
	Work schedules
	Wage rate (if all employees are for same job)
	Probation period
	Breaks
	Pay Days, Vacation/Personal Days/Bonus Days

11:00 a.m.	**Employee Hire Package (0.25)** **H/R**
	Hire form

	TD 1
	Direct deposit
	Induction form (have employee check off items as covered)
	Emergency contact information
11:15 a.m.	**Benefits (0.25)** **H/R**
	Outline coverage
	Outline eligibility
	Fill out the necessary forms for submission at end of probation
11:30 a.m.	**Policies and Procedures (0.5)** **H/R**
	Sign-off policies
	Attendance guidelines, parking, dress code, supplies
	Safety, hygiene and good housekeeping guidelines
	Harassment policy
	E-mail use and phone calls
	Substance-abuse policy
	Attendance-control program
	Recognition policy
	Contractor and visitor policies
	Feedback/staff relations box and team philosophy
12:00 p.m.	**Lunch (0.5)**

12:30 p.m.	**Main Safety Rules/OH&S Policies (0.25)** **Safety/Supervisor**
	Safety slogan
	Reporting hazards
	Reporting injuries
	Personal protective equipment
	Forklift policy
12:45 p.m.	**Safety Plant Tour (1.5)** **Safety/Supervisor**
	First Aid room
	How to summon first aid
	Fire prevention/exits
	Eye wash stations
	Personal protective equipment
	Introduce lock-outs
	Evacuation procedures
	Ozone
	Map of plant
2:15 p.m.	**Meet the Department Manager (0.25)**
	Department's philosophy
	Open-door policy
2:30 p.m.	**Break (0.25)**

2:45 p.m.	"Company" Team Challenge Game (0.25) H/R and Supervisor
	Split into teams and answer questions
	Name of the Plant Director.
	What is WHMIS?
	Name two crucial elements of the attendance guidelines.
	What is the telephone policy?
	Name two ways to get resolution to a problem.
	What do you do to a machine before you try any repairs?
	Name two different machines on the production line.
	Give an example of personal protective equipment worn in the plant.
	Give two examples of behavior that could be considered harassment.
	When are you entitled to benefit coverage?
	All participants receive a company shirt.
3:00 p.m.	**WHMIS (1.25)** **Safety**
	Dangerous material—introduction video
	Quiz – participants receive a company sweatshirt
4:15 p.m.	**Communication/Computer System (0.25)** **IT**
	Voice mail/e-mail and computer

4:30 p.m.	**Wrap-Up**
	H/R & Supervisor
	Next steps—introduce company training program

An effective orientation program, or the lack of one, will make a significant difference in how quickly a new employee becomes productive and feels part of the team. Make sure your new employees feel that they are valued and that you want them to come back the next day, and the day after that, and the day after that.

EMPLOYEE TRAINING AND DEVELOPMENT

Retaining high-quality employees means making a commitment to them that you will do what you can to keep their skills current and relevant, and that you will work with them to fully develop their professional potential. This means offering specific skill training as well as personal development training. So while it is important to train employees on new technology that is introduced, it is equally important to train them to communicate effectively, work together as a team, become supervisors or managers and become better, all-around employees.

There is a myriad of training opportunities available from customized in-house training to workshops and seminars to video series to books and audiotapes. The list is endless and the cost limitless, unfortunately our training budgets do have limits and sometimes quite tight ones. However tight you think your training budget is, though, the payoffs in terms of return on investment are undeniable. Study after study and survey after survey show that commitment to employee training increases workplace productivity and job satisfaction. Regardless of the amount you have to spend on employee training, the basics are the same.

Retaining high-quality employees means keeping their skills current and relevant, working with them to fully develop their professional potential, and offering specific skill training as well as personal development training.

Why Develop and Train Employees?

Training and development is initiated for a variety of reasons for an employee or group of employees. Typical reasons include:

- When a performance appraisal indicates performance improvement is needed.

- To "benchmark" the status of improvement so far in a performance-improvement effort.

- As part of an overall professional development program.

- As part of succession planning to help an employee be eligible for a planned change in role in the organization.

- To "pilot," or test, the operation of a new performance management system.

- To train about a specific topic.

Common Topics of Employee Training

- **Communications:** The increasing diversity of today's workforce brings a wide variety of languages and customs.

- **Computer skills:** Computer skills are becoming necessary for all staff, not just administrative and office positions.

- **Customer service:** Increased competition in today's global marketplace makes it critical that employees understand and meet the needs of customers.

- **Diversity:** Diversity training usually includes explanation about how people have different perspectives and views and includes techniques to value diversity.

- **Ethics:** Today's society has increasing expectations about corporate social responsibility. Also, today's diverse workforce brings a wide variety of values and morals to the workplace.

- **Human relations:** The increased stresses of today's workplace can include misunderstandings and conflict. Training can help people to get along in the workplace.

- **Quality initiatives:** Initiatives such as Total Quality Management, Six Sigma, benchmarking, etc., require basic training about quality concepts, guidelines and standards for quality, etc.

- **Safety:** Safety training is critical when working with heavy equipment, hazardous chemicals, repetitive activities, etc., but can also be useful with practical advice for avoiding assaults, etc.

- **Sexual harassment:** Sexual harassment training usually includes careful description of the organization's policies about sexual harassment, especially about what are inappropriate behaviors.

General Benefits from Employee Training and Development

There are numerous sources of information about training and development and they suggest several compelling reasons for management to commit to training employees. These reasons include:

- Increased job satisfaction and morale among employees.

- Increased employee motivation.

- Increased efficiencies in processes resulting in financial gain.

- Increased capacity to adopt new technologies and methods.

- Increased innovation in strategies and products.

- Reduced employee turnover.

- Enhanced company image; e.g., conducting ethics training.

- Risk management; e.g., training about sexual harassment, diversity training.

Principles of Effective Training

Training is a dynamic process made up of four major components: 1) planning and support, 2) needs assessment, 3) methods and activities, and 4) evaluation and feedback. Training experts suggest that companies should continuously plan for and support training that is linked to their mission, goals and objectives; assess current and future training needs of all employees; ensure that appropriate training activities are provided; and evaluate and utilize the results. The following model emphasizes those four elements.

1. Planning and Support

- Develop policies communicating the significance of training.

- Develop training plans.

- Set minimum training requirements for all employees.

- Develop procedures to implement training policies.

- Communicate training information to all employees.

- Support training with funds and staff.

- Ensure employees responsible for training have adequate skills.

Businesses must have a clear vision of their roles and responsibilities and the human resources necessary to attain them. Although training is only one of many tools available to management, its link to agency performance should be clearly delineated, communicated and supported at all levels within an organization. Seven principles, which are summarized below, demonstrate management support for training and help lay the necessary foundation for its success.

2. Needs Assessment

- Identify agency's core competencies.

- Identify competency gaps.

- Monitor performance.

- Involve employees in identifying training needs.

- Develop individual training plans.

- Identify training opportunities.

- Set training priorities.

Training efforts should be targeted toward your business's core skill requirements so that they can achieve their mission, goals and objectives. To help ensure this, you need to routinely identify deficiencies by comparing the competencies that have been identified as necessary to achieve their mission, goals and objectives with employees' knowledge, skills and abilities. Performance should also be routinely monitored to identify problems that may be addressed by training.

3. Methods and Activities

- Ensure that training activities are relevant to agency's goals.

- Use a variety of training methods.

- Provide training as efficiently as possible.

- Make training accessible.

It is important to identify and provide access to training activities that narrow skill gaps and address performance problems identified in needs assessment. These four training principles encourage businesses to use diverse and efficient methods to provide training activities that are linked to their mission, goals and objectives. This includes collaborating with businesses to provide training as efficiently as possible.

4. Evaluation and Feedback

- Maintain training records.

- Link training to employee performance.

- Evaluate the effectiveness of training.

- Use evaluation results to modify training methods and activities.

- Use evaluation results to monitor business plans and goals.

Not only should evaluation measure participant reactions to individual training sessions, but it should also try to measure changes in learning, job behavior and organizational performance whenever possible.

TRAINING IDEAS AND SUGGESTIONS

It is important to develop innovative and cost-effective ways to train. Because traditional instructor-led classroom training is expensive and inappropriate for some workplaces, it is important to use other models and unique activities. Here are some low-cost alternatives:

Train the Trainer

Assign an appropriate employee to attend training workshops or seminars, then have that employee teach everyone else. Choose the right person to attend specific programs and then make it his or her responsibility to teach others.

Take Online Courses

Distance learning or Web-based corporate training is exploding lately. There are now dozens of affordable

There are many continuing education and even degree programs that can be done on the Internet; continuous learning is accessible to everyone, and with a little company support, it is very attractive.

offerings and options. Training can be done in real-time by linking people in many places together. This saves travel and other related expenses. Many online courses can be downloaded or accessed whenever an employee chooses — this means it can be done in the office and employees can work at their own pace. There are many continuing education and even degree programs that can be done on the Internet; continuous learning is accessible to everyone, and with a little company support, it is very attractive.

Share the Cost

Set up training sessions in a public venue and then invite other small-business owners to buy seats. Recruit partner companies and set up classes with open enrollment so staffers from any participating company can register.

Set up training sessions in a public venue and then invite other small-business owners.

Access All Training Sources

Audiotapes and books are cheap, effective and reliable methods to deliver training.

The Murder Mystery Game

This popular social activity can be brought into the workplace to develop a variety of operational skills. Everyone contributes to solving the murder; they must identify the victim, the murder weapon, the time and place of the murder, the murderer, and the motive. The cost is very little and it only requires an hour or so of employee time. It is fun

and unexpected, and it address a variety of training issues
including:

- Making discussions more productive.

- Enhancing problem-solving skills.

- Increasing clarity of communications.

- Discovering productive team behaviors.

- Improving listening and questioning skills.

- Adding participation and involvement.

- Increasing awareness of the contributions of others.

Host an Employee "Rap" Session

Get your employees together to create a rap song that
addresses an issue relevant to the workplace. Encourage
humor and outrageousness and let the creative juices flow.
It is a fun, team-building event that improves morale and
breaks up the monotony of work. Here is a Rap on Stress that
was posted on the Internet by the Stress Doc (www.stressdoc.
com).

When it comes to feelings do you stuff them inside?
Is tough John Wayne your emotional guide?
And it's not just men so proud and tight-lipped.
For every Rambo there seems to be a Rambette.

So you give up sleep, become wired and spent

Escape lonely frustration as a mal-content.
It's time to look at your style of stress.
You can't just dress or undress for success.

Are you grouchy with colleagues or quietly mean?
Hell, you'd rather talk to your computer machine.
When the telephone rings, you're under the gun
Now you could reach out and really crush someone.

The boss makes demands yet gives little control
So you prey on chocolate and wish life were dull,
But Office desk's a mess, often skipping meals
Inside your car looks like a pocketbook on wheels.
Those deadlines, deadlines . . . all that aggravation
Whew, you only have time for procrastination.
Now I made you feel guilty, you want to confess
Better you should practice
"The Art of Safe Stress."

Discussion and Drawing Exercise

Get employees to divide into groups of four. Ask them to
brainstorm ideas that address one of the training issues
identified as necessary, such as, "How can we improve
interpersonal communication in our office?" Then the teams
are challenged to design a group picture that pulls together
their individual ideas during the collective brainstorm.
The picture should be some kind of symbol or tell a story.
Provide large flip chart paper and markers and let the
drawing begin. Point out that there are no marks for drawing
technique and that stick figures are allowed. Encourage the
outrageous, and as the drawing evolves, the groups get more
and more enthused and they love "showing and telling"

Brainstorm ideas that address one of the training issues identified. Provide large flip chart paper and markers and let the drawing begin.

their masterpieces. Hang the creations in the lunchroom and I guarantee they will elicit more response than the tired and tedious motivational posters that so many of us feel compelled to buy.

Role Play

Have groups of employees enact skits depicting workplace issues. The ideas generated create a wonderful learning and sharing forum. These role-plays are especially instructive and effective when the workplace issue involves interpersonal conflict. Role-plays are great mediums for acting out frustration and anger (passive or explosive) and generating group problem-solving while modeling good communication and conflict resolution skills. The role-plays are most valuable when all levels of the organization (managers and supervisors) and a broad range of employee groups (production, sales and clerical) are represented. Again, the listening and learning is only outdone by the audience laughter. You may even want to videotape the skits and distribute them in the workplace; all employees willing of course.

The lesson for employee training and development is to customize and be creative. Every workplace is different and each employee is different. Do what is best for your employees and they will do what is best for you. It does not take a huge cash outlay to convince employees that you are concerned about their professional development; what it takes is a commitment to make training a priority and then a follow-through on that commitment.

CHAPTER 5

MOTIVATION
Creating Job Satisfaction

"As long as you're green, you're growing.
As soon as you're ripe, you start to rot."
—Ray Kroc

While it is important to attend to the training and support needs of your employees and to be actively involved in recruiting and hiring people who fit your organization, effective managers devote much of their time to motivating their employees to perform over and above the required minimums. A well-rounded motivation strategy integrates performance and satisfaction. This means that while it is important for employees to feel good about what they are doing and feel appreciated, it is still necessary to hold them accountable for results. The best companies have productive people who are satisfied with their work environment and who are committed to the company's success.

WHAT IS MOTIVATION?

In order to understand motivation, we need to break it down into three distinct and interrelated parts.

The first aspect of motivation involves satisfying one's needs: Motivation towards better performance depends on the satisfaction of needs for responsibility, achievement, recognition and growth.

The second aspect of motivation is that needs are always changing: Needs are felt, and their intensity varies from one person to another and from time to time, and so does the extent to which they are motivating.

Thirdly, motivated behavior can be reinforced: Behavior is learned, and earned reward encourages even better performance, thus reinforcing desired behavior.

Motivation is a very complex topic, but, essentially, if we know what people need and want, then we know what they will work for, and if we reinforce them for their performance, they will continue to work well and achieve.

We all have needs, and according to Maslow's Hierarchy of Needs theory, they range from the most basic of physiological needs (food and shelter) to the need for self-fulfillment. When we choose to work, we are doing it because we need to earn money to survive, so working in and of itself satisfies a basic need. So, at a very deep level, we are motivated to work, period, but the contextual factors related to our work environment provide further motivation to do a good job. These factors include the physical work environment (temperature, comfort, arrangement, noise, aesthetics, safety, etc.) and the employment conditions (salary, benefits, supervision, policies, job status, job security, etc.).

Maslow's Hierarchy of Needs

These "maintenance factors," as Hertberg calls them, are important and necessary to providing the kind of work environment that attracts employees in the first place. These factors can be viewed as base-line requirements for a healthy workplace, and hopefully we've gotten to the point where most companies can offer a good base level of satisfaction. But a good or average base is not enough to keep the best people in your organization — they are looking for, and deserve, more from their work. In order to retain your top staff, you need to foster a culture and environment that values your employees and allows and encourages them to reach their potential.

This type of organization goes beyond basic needs and recognizes that people need to feel appreciated and recognized for their contributions, and these are the types of social, ego and self-fulfilling needs that have real motivating potential. The things that motivate on the job include:

- Achievement

- Recognition

- Work itself

- Advancement

- Responsibility

- Possibility of growth

Employee Motivation Program

In order to effect a successful motivation program, you must start with the following assumptions:

- Employees start out motivated. A lack of motivation is a learned response fostered by misunderstood or unrealistic expectations.

- Management is responsible for creating a supportive, problem-solving work environment in which necessary resources to perform a task are provided.

- Rewards should encourage high personal performance that is consistent with management objectives.

- Motivation works best when it is based on self-governance.

- Employees need to be treated fairly and consistently.

- Employees deserve timely, honest feedback on their work performance.

The onus is on mangers to create a motivating environment and continuously monitor the situation to ensure it evolves and stays motivating.

RULES OF EMPLOYEE MOTIVATION

Define Expectations

The foundation of an effective motivation program is proper goal-setting. Do your employees understand their role in the organization? Do they see a connection between their daily duties and the bottom line? Unless the answer is yes to both of those questions, then they are simply showing up and collecting a paycheck.

It is very important for employees to feel ownership and empowerment, and this happens when they have goals to achieve that are tied to operational performance. These are called performance goals, and the best way to achieve them is to make them SMART. SMART goals are:

- **Specific:** well-defined and clear to all parties.

- **Measurable:** you know if the goal is obtainable, how far away completion is, and when it has been achieved.

- **Achievable:** it should be something that is challenging but also within your ability to attain.

- **Realistic:** within the availability of resources, knowledge and time.

- **Time-framed:** set a start and end date, leave enough time to achieve the goal within realistic parameters.

Examples of SMART Goals	
Reduce finished product defects by 15 percent next quarter.	Respond to employee suggestions within 48 hours of receipt.

Telling a person to take initiative or do their best is not motivating because these terms mean different things to different people. SMART goals are agreed upon and readily verifiable and quantifiable.

Increase the Value of Work

In order to make something motivating, it is important to find out what is important to your employees. Most people think that money is the main motivator but that is actually not the case. Different people are motivated by different things at different times, and the best way to find out what employees value is to ask them directly. Companies have spent thousands of dollars on recognition programs only to find out that the reward is a joke to the staff; instead of getting a company t-shirt, what they really wanted was a company picnic table out back. Here are some examples of things commonly considered valuable:

Flexible Schedules

Options include employees working more hours on certain days and fewer on others, in fixed or variable schedules. Compressed work weeks offer employees the opportunity to bundle two full weeks of full-time work into a fixed schedule of eight or nine days. In all circumstances, the programs are structured to meet business objectives while recognizing individual needs.

Job Sharing

Two or more people splitting position responsibilities is another way to acknowledge personal needs while bringing diversity of experience to a singular position. Individuals sharing jobs and working part-time may potentially reduce benefit costs while retaining talent that may otherwise choose to retire or leave the company. Factors to consider are the need to communicate between position participants and the transferability of knowledge.

Loyalty and productivity may be enhanced in telecommuting situations.

Telecommuting

Employees with high motivation, self-discipline, necessary skills and independent orientation are ideal candidates to work off-site. Loyalty and productivity may be enhanced in telecommuting situations; however, companies should have mechanisms in place to measure the success and contributions of telecommuting workers.

Paid Leave Banks

A structured program that combines vacation, short-term sick leave, personal days and emergency leave is a way to reward and motivate employees. Although the company retains the right to grant approval for leave, the employee can accrue more discretionary days than with some traditional programs. The costs remain the same for the company, while participants perceive greater control and are more likely to remain contented in the long run.

Phased Retirement

By offering a combination of pension modification and staggered working periods, a program can be structured to reduce overall expenses, motivate and retain the employee and help meet business objectives.

Developmental Opportunities and Career Planning

Many individuals express frustration in performing the same responsibilities over and over. The ability of a company to structure career-planning programs, including job rotations, skills training and project management assignments, are of interest to many employees. Providing opportunities to learn new technologies and methods and accomplish new achievements is significant in capturing prolonged interest from high-potential staff. Giving people the opportunity to gain exposure and implement new programs while building self-esteem and credibility is valuable for both the company and the employee. If an assignment increases their value on the job market, it is very motivating, and ongoing training, especially in technological skills, is often a requirement for employment. Opportunity and recognition of accomplishments can prove to be a much more lucrative incentive than any financial considerations a company may offer.

Sabbaticals

Providing a mid-career break to refresh and rejuvenate is exactly what some employees are looking for. Sabbaticals can be an effective means of energizing these workers.

Feedback

People crave knowing what other people think of their work. Although autonomy is important, so is ready access to and abundant time with managers.

Tangible Rewards

Small and immediate, concrete, tangible rewards, such as money, dinner certificates and tickets to cultural events, are very motivating. The key here is to find out what events or activities motivate the employee. Just because you like to watch the game from the corporate box seat does not mean that your accountant feels the same way.

Have Fun

For well-balanced individuals, their personal lives are more important than their careers. Incentives and benefits that demonstrate an organization's support of a balance are attractive to them.

Pat People on the Back

Few perks are cheaper, easier or more effective than recognition. Recognition can take a variety of forms. The basic premise is to catch people doing something right and then tell them and others about it.

Share the Perks of Your Business

Is there an aspect of your business that you could turn into an inexpensive employee benefit? Maybe you get merchandise or certificates from suppliers. Instead of keeping those for the managers, share

Incentives that demonstrate an organization's support of a balance between personal and professional life are attractive to many employees.

them with your top performers. Don't forget to let employees share in perks you provide to your clients.

Feed Employees' Bodies

What is the easiest way to an employee's heart? Through the

proverbial stomach! Provide monthly in-house luncheons, order pizza on a Friday afternoon or bake a cake for each employee's birthday. These are fun events that encourage intermingling and foster loyalty.

Feed Employees' Souls

Give employees time off to perform community service. Employees who otherwise do not have the time to volunteer at local schools or work with teens or canvas for a charity can do the work that gives back. Offer a wellness program where you reimburse employees, up to a certain amount, for anything they related to their spiritual, mental or physical well-being.

Offer Advancement Opportunities

One of the best incentives for ambitious people is opportunity. Fill management positions by promoting from within, ensuring that long-term employees have a chance to rise, and that new employees have an incentive to stay.

Provide Support

In order for people to be motivated, you must set the groundwork by offering a supportive work environment. No amount of goal-setting or original rewards will work if your employees don't feel they are being given the resources and materials necessary for success. You must ask yourself, "Do my employees feel it is possible to achieve this goal?" Support means providing resources, training and encouragement; essentially, managers need to pave the way for success.

It is important to take this concept beyond lip-service and really commit to supporting your employees. Support comes back to the notion of validation; if an employee does not feel they have been given the tools necessary to succeed, then they will naturally feel invalidated and unworthy. Nothing is more unmotivating than the feeling of helplessness and being sent out to sink or swim. From your first day of orientation to the employee's last day on the job, you must provide all the information, background, training and encouragement necessary to be successful. Employees need to feel that management is working hard to help them achieve their performance goals.

Give Feedback

Once a goal has been established and agreed upon, employees need to have access to how they are progressing. Once a year at performance review time is not enough, nor is it

Weekly or monthly progress reports are good ways to establish feedback controls.

even remotely adequate. People need to know how they are doing — good and bad; and by setting SMART goals, they have a tangible way to measure their progress. Spontaneous feedback is excellent and provides an immediate boost, but feedback also needs to be given formally. The process does not have to be overly time-consuming or overly rigid, it simply needs to take place at regular intervals.

Weekly or monthly progress reports are good ways to establish feedback controls. This ensures that timely praise is given and performance coaching can be done before the problem spins out of control. Brief, frequent and highly visible feedback is the kind that motivates, and managers should look for some opportunity to praise their employees every week. Study after study has shown that praise and recognition tend to build employee loyalty. People want to feel that what they do makes a difference, and money alone does not do this; personal recognition does.

No-Cost Ways to Recognize and Praise Employees
Provide Information

Information is power, and employees want to be empowered with the information they need to know to do their jobs better and more effectively. And, more than ever, employees want to know how they are doing in their jobs and how the company is doing in its business. Open the channels of communication in your organization to allow employees to be informed, ask questions and share information.

Encourage Involvement

Managers today are faced with an incredible number of opportunities and problems and, as the speed of business continues to increase dramatically, the amount of time that they have to make decisions continues to decrease. Involving employees in decision-making, especially when the decisions affect them directly, is both respectful and practical. Those closest to the problem typically have the best insight as to what to do. As you involve others, you increase their commitment and ease in implementing new ideas or change.

Foster Independence

Few employees want their every action to be closely monitored. Most employees appreciate having the flexibility to do their jobs as they see fit. Giving people latitude increases the chance that they will perform as you desire — and bring additional initiative, ideas and energy to their jobs.

Increase Visibility

Everyone appreciates getting credit when it is due. Occasions to share the successes of employees with others are almost limitless. Giving employees new opportunities to perform, learn and grow as a form of recognition and thanks is highly motivating for most people.

Reward Success

Like feedback, rewards for success must be given in a timely manner. Rewards, even highly valuable ones, lose their motivating potential unless they are given at the correct time. It is the timing of reinforcements that lets employees know which behaviors are being encouraged. While this seems quite obvious, it is often not done — after going through all the administration required, their reward is sometimes not actually given for weeks after the fact. Delay between performance and feedback dilutes the effectiveness of the reward so it is imperative that you be prepared with your system of motivation and plan ahead for the administration aspects.

It is also important to reward success consistently and fairly. There is nothing more demotivating than a reward that is given under unfair circumstances or out of preferential treatment (perceived or otherwise). Establish the parameters of your reward system and treat all employees with the same rules. Again, this seems obvious but it is very easy to reward Bob "just this one time" even though he was off his goal slightly. "After all, he is usually the top performer and he just had a bad month; we wouldn't want to upset him or anything. The other guys will understand." The intent is honorable, but the effect can be devastating if the other guys don't understand, and you have sacrificed many people for the sake of one.

Although this example may seem petty on the surface, it is this type of inconsistency in a workplace that fester and create toxic work environments. This is not to say that common sense and good judgment are thrown away for the sake of absolute fairness, but it does mean that you must think of all the ramifications of bending the rules ever so slightly.

"Any business or industry that pays equal rewards to its goof-offs and its eager-beavers sooner or later will find itself with more goof-offs than eager-beavers."
—Mick Delaney

Motivation Boosters	Motivation Deflators
Responsibility	Meaningless, repetitive work
Meaningful work	Confusion
Variety in assignments	Lack of trust
Measurable outputs	No input in decisions
Challenge	Not knowing what's going on
Solving problems	Not knowing how well you are doing
Trust	Someone solving problems for you
Participation in decisions	No time to solve problems
Ability to measure own performance	Across-the-board rules and regulations
Being listened to	Not getting credit for your ideas or efforts
Praise	Lack of resources, knowledge, skills and coaching
Recognition for contributions	Inconsistency

HOW TO MAINTAIN GOOD EMPLOYEE RELATIONS

The following are tips that all employers can use to maintain good employee relations. Management attitudes create the culture of an organization. The following tips can be applied to create a culture that is satisfying to employees and productive for the organization.

Be Knowledgeable of Employment Laws

Wages and compensation are always important to employees. Be aware of local, state and federal laws governing pay rates. For example, in 2004 the Department of Labor enacted new rules regarding "white-collar" employees and overtime-pay requirements. Employers can obtain a copy of the regulations and other information about the new rules at www.dol.gov /fairpay.

Be Available for Discussion of Employee Problems

Let employees know that they can go to management with problems and concerns. Ensure that management conduct creates an environment of trust and confidence. Managers must take concerns seriously and address them promptly. Don't put people off; they won't forget it!

Maintain Confidentiality

When employees discuss matters of concern to management, their confidences must be respected. When confidences must be shared to resolve the problem, the employee should be told.

Give Uninterrupted Attention to Employees

Don't allow visitors and phone calls when discussing an important matter with employees. Let your actions convey that the employee is important to you. Give employees the focused attention they deserve.

Conduct Well-Organized Meetings

Meetings should provide valuable information and solicit employee feedback. Whenever possible, try to avoid surprises in the agenda.

Don't Criticize Employees in Public

If an employee must be corrected, do so privately. Never point out an employee's mistakes to or in front of other employees.

Coach, Rather Than Criticize

When corrective action is necessary, be timely, clear and accurate. Provide the employee with concrete examples to ensure that he or she understands the problem so that they can improve the performance.

Treat Employees Equally

Perceptions of special treatment can be extremely damaging to morale, as well as creating potential legal liability.

Remember the Little Things

Birthdays, company anniversaries and special events, and give recognition when due.

Encourage Staff Input

Share problems and challenges wherever appropriate and ask for suggestions on how best to deal with it.

Delegate and Develop

Delegate new, challenging tasks to employees. Provide opportunities for employees to develop new skills.

Welcome Change

Welcome change as a means by which you, your employees and the company can progress to a better future. Generate enthusiasm for change.

Support Organizational Goals

Work as a team, ensuring there are no interdepartmental battlegrounds that are counterproductive.

Be Human

Enjoy your work and employees and share your enthusiasm. Make yourself approachable and willing to listen.

PERFORMANCE MANAGEMENT

A key part of any manager's or supervisor's job is improving employee performance. Whether this means bringing unsatisfactory performance up to acceptable minimums or helping outstanding employees reach their full potential, the methods are the same and should be applied equitably across all staff. You might seek ways to motivate the employee, provide further training, redesign the job, or even change supervision tactics. While these approaches are all good, the basic, and often forgotten, principle underlying performance management is: Employees can't perform up to their full capabilities unless they (1) know what the standards of performance are for their job, and (2) know how well they are meeting those standards. These factors are the most important determinants of performance and most supervisors handle the first element quite well.

Supervisors are regularly encouraged and rewarded for establishing performance standards and instructing employees in the task to be done to improve quality and quantity of output. It is the second element, the providing of appropriate feedback, that presents the most difficulty for supervisors. Performance appraisal, or letting employees know where they stand and how well they are doing, is so critical and so often not done or done very poorly.

When an employee is already performing well, appraisal is easy. Even the most jaded supervisor can be convinced to give compliments and praise at least once in a while. The problem arises when the employee's performance is not satisfactory and must be improved. This is where special skill and tact come into play and where many supervisors balk at the responsibility.

THE PERFORMANCE CYCLE

What you need to do to manage employee performance effectively is treat the process as an ongoing cycle of planning, focusing and assessing. People need to know what's expected of them in their job. A job is only a job unless it has meaning and is derived from purpose. To accomplish this, mangers must ensure that:

- Expectations are spelled out it plain language.

- Employees have the competence to do the job.

- Organizational goals help employees achieve their own goals.

- Coaching for success is done on a regular basis.

- There is openness to discussion and input.

- Feedback is timely and effective.

- Distinctive recognition for success takes place.

It is particularly vital to establish an expectation of success within your workplace and get employee commitment to achieving this success. This can be done with the three-stage performance process:

PERFORMANCE PLANNING
PERFORMANCE FOCUSING
PERFORMANCE ASSESSMENT

When an organization's strategic direction and goals have been developed and communicated, the employees can focus on the work at hand. Employees know how they contribute to the overall success of the company and they know exactly what is expected of them. They know this because the strategy has been clearly communicated and their managers and supervisors have worked with them to develop SMART goals that support the corporate strategy. If there is no clearly articulated strategy or objectives, individual departments and employees work independent of one another, and not necessarily in the same direction. The purpose of planning is to increase the probability that employees will achieve the desired results with the resources they are given.

Performance Planning

This stage involves developing or revising an inventory of key results for each job. This means defining the job's purpose, listing the key results areas, and setting performance indicators. The five elements of a performance inventory are:

1. The job's key result areas.

Maintain manufacturing equipment.

2. The job's performance indicators.
   Manufacturing equipment is in good repair and reliable.

3. Measurable targets and standards.
   Reduce manufacturing downtime by 10 percent.

4. Performance consequences.
   Contribute to operational efficiency and improve profitability.

5. Training plan.
   Send employee on manufacturer training courses when new machines or upgrades are installed.

Remember, this plan deals with the "job" not the "job holder," so the performance inventory is the same no matter who is in the position.

Performance Focusing

This is the longest stage and involves monitoring performance, reinforcing success, counseling, coaching, mentoring and tutoring. It means confronting and diagnosing performance problems and jointly developing solutions. Discussion about performance is ongoing between all parties and documenting these discussions is very important. The reasons for documenting are numerous:

- To provide an ongoing factual record of an employee's performance.

- To identify an employee's strengths so they can be better utilized and developed.

- To identify an employee's weakness so they can be overcome.

- To identify training needs.

- To clarify performance problems so corrective action can be taken in a timely manner.

- To accumulate as much relevant and accurate information as possible in order to have a complete picture of the employee's performance before making decisions on promotion, demotion, transfers and termination.

- To act as a memory jogger for the manger or supervisor.

- To provide accurate data to base disciplinary action and support those actions if necessary.

While the process of documentation may seem cumbersome at first, its value is immeasurable when an employee initiates a wrongful dismissal action or grievance.

How and What to Document

At the very minimum you need to include the following information:

- When did the incident occur?

- Who was involved?
- What happened?
- What action was taken?

Document immediately

You will forget or omit facts later, and this will decrease your credibility if ever questioned.

Use observation vs. inference

Write down what actually happened, observable and defendable information, and is not open to interpretation. For example, if an employee is late four days in a row, write down, "Janice was late four days in a row February 13–16" rather than, "Janice is irresponsible and shows no concern for her job."

Include existing conditions

This information helps you to recall an incident if questioned about it some time in the future. It also provides contextual clues for why a person may be behaving poorly. Does the behavior always crop up when change is happening or when deadlines are looming? Some example include:

- Immediate deadlines
- Time period
- Work level
- Stress level
- Number of employees working together on a project
- Organizational policies or procedures

Documentation is vital for effective performance management and assessment. It helps all parties accurately discuss the situation and work toward acceptable solutions.

Performance Assessment

When we think of the typical performance assessment, we think of the most unmotivating, uncomfortable, unproductive hour of our work year. The manager is stumbling trying to find nice ways to tell the employee his or her performance was average, and all that the employee wants is to hear is that his or her average performance earned a perfunctory wage increase of 3 percent. Better yet, the manager sees this time as the perfect opportunity to ambush his employee; chastising her for the way she deals with customers and coworkers, signing her up for an Effective Communication workshop, and then linking her 3 percent raise with her new positive attitude. This does not, and should not, be the case. Done correctly, performance reviews are a prime source of employee motivation and relationship-building.

Done correctly, performance reviews are a prime source of employee motivation and relationship-building.

TYPICAL PERFORMANCE REVIEW SHEET

Name: *Art Average*

Date: *Dec 31, 2003*

Performance Factors

1. Job Knowledge
   Shows acceptable knowledge

2. Quality/Productivity
   Poor use of time, quality OK

3. Interpersonal Relations
   Gets along OK

4. Dependability
   Never know where you are

5. Salary Review
   3.8% wage adjustment approved

_____
Mandy Manager
Signature of Manager

_____
Art Average
Signature of Employee

Effective Performance Assessment

In this final stage of the performance cycle, you summarize the documentation, prepare a formal summary, make compensation recommendations, and discuss the employee's future. This discussion is planned and both parties are prepared for the exchange. If the employee's performance is monitored effectively, there is no reason for any information in the assessment to be a surprise; this is simply a time set aside to look at the work period as a whole and discuss opportunities for employee development. The purpose of the discussion is to discover how and why the person is performing on the job and how the organization can aid his or her development so that both parties benefit.

Performance assessment maintains and improves an employee's performance and motivation by:

- Reviewing, summarizing and confirming the information that was developed during the assessment period.

- Increasing self-awareness of strengths and weaknesses that affect performance.

- Creating specific plans for personal development.

- Improving communication and commitment.

- Maintaining and improving performance by clarifying expectation and setting SMART goals.

- Recognizing and acknowledging achievement.

To develop the plan, you must work closely with the employee to determine how he or she can best contribute to the businesses objectives and help the organization as a whole.

Characteristics of a Positive Performance Review

- Gain better understanding of your employees.

- Use honest, open communication.

- Provide clear expectations.

- Discuss any misunderstandings that may have occurred.

- Showcase achievements.

- Define SMART goals.

- Develop an action plan to achieve those goals.

- Identify areas of conflict or discord and make a plan to address.

- Provide positive feedback.

- Give employees an opportunity to open up and vent.

- Forum to talk candidly about areas for improvement and make a commitment to actually implement.

- Opportunity to learn about employee's long-term goals.

- Formal documentation of achievements.

- No surprises — this is a summary recap, not a one-and-only conversation.

Although official performance assessments are usually conducted annually, performance must be managed on a day-to-day, week-to-week, month-to-month basis if individuals in an organization are to achieve superior performance. If performance management and superior results are to be achieved, an organization must have a strong performance ethic. This means the culture must support performance reviews as the key way to maintain a good employment relationship; open communication and a high degree of trust and mutual respect exemplify this ethic.

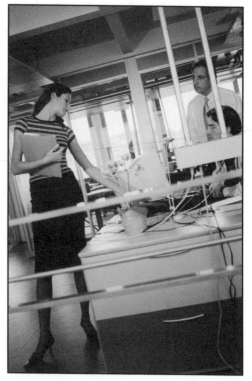

Managers must provide coaching when it's necessary and monitor employees' performance daily.

Effective individuals in organizations with a performance

ethic have opportunities to influence outcomes by providing input, making decisions and implanting them, and collaborating with their managers. Managers provide coaching when it's necessary and monitor employees' performance daily. Employees can readily seek out their manager for advice or assistance or if they have ideas to contribute; the whole work process is a collaborative effort.

Conducting a Performance Interview

Giving and receiving is integral to an effective performance review process. The purpose of the review is to discuss the employee's performance and facilitate growth, both personally and professionally. The fundamental principle underlying performance reviews is open and honest communication—this means that the employee is as much a part of the review as the manager is. It is not a one-way process where the manager delivers a verdict on the employee, the employee agrees to work on stated deficiencies and then the compensation level is evaluated.

A performance review is not a necessary evil; it is a prime opportunity to build trust and develop loyalty. How do you do this? There are four phases to employee assessment:

Preparatory Planning

This is where the review process is communicated. Many companies have instituted reciprocal review systems where the employee has an opportunity to review his or her manager or supervisor's performance in activities that directly affect that employee's performance. These are often referred to as 360 reviews, and they can be very useful and insightful when used correctly and when used within a corporate culture of high trust and respect. Another way to include your employees more fully in the review process is to have them review their own performance. Typically, employees are given the same review sheet that their manager uses, and employees are required to bring their self-assessment to the performance interview.

Because performance reviews should not be surprising to anyone, casually comparing the two reviews is an excellent way to start the discussion, and it reveals some interesting facts about where employees feel their own strengths and weaknesses are. You'll be surprised that employees don't elevate their scores and often they assess their performance below your ratings — this presents the perfect opportunity to praise and recognize your employees in ways they don't expect. The cardinal rule is for nothing in the review to be a surprise, so the more time spent in preparation and actually performance coaching on a daily basis, the better.

Discussion Initiation
The moment has arrived and now it is up to the manger to set the tone for the meeting. No matter how prepared the parties are, performance reviews are always stressful. Set the climate, try to relax the person and reassure him or her that nothing unexpected is going to transpire.

Conduct the Interview
Use direct and open communication throughout the process. When discussing performance problems, relate the discussion to performance expectations. This reinforces the need to have set goals and clear expectations from the start. It is very difficult to assess an employee's performance if you

have never sat down to discuss exactly what you expect. Where necessary, have your documentation handy to jog both of your memories about specific incidents, and detail the positive and negative aspects using the evidence given. Focus on the behavior, not the person; give praise when it is deserved and acknowledge your employee's reactions and comments.

This is a two-way conversation, and it is important to get your employee's perspective on the issues as well. This means listening closely to what interests them, what they value, what they see as good performance and what causes them frustration and stress. The ultimate goal of the dialogue is to come to a better understanding of each other and then make a plan to develop and grow in ways that are beneficial to the company.

Closing

This is where you negotiate for change. The negotiation process involves coming to an agreement on any issues that exist, and then developing a solid action plan to address the problem. Goal-setting is important in this process, and remember the SMART principles: specific, measurable, achievable, realistic and time-framed. Create the plan together and then commit to monitoring it. Discuss the progress of goals made in the last review and amend them, conclude them and make new ones. End the discussion with positives, recognizing successes and achievements, and always leave the door open for future discussion. Assessment is an on-going, dynamic process and, when viewed positively, it is invaluable to the organization and its employees.

SAMPLE PERFORMANCE REVIEW

Name: _____

Position: _____

Appraiser: _____ Date: _____

List major duties and performance expectations in the spaces below, check the applicable rating and comment.

1—Exceptional   2—Exceeds expectations   3—Meets expectations
4—Improvement required   5—Unacceptable

Key Result Area
Performance Expectations
Performance Evaluation
Rating 1 2 3 4 5
Comments

Key Result Area
Performance Expectations
Performance Evaluation
Rating 1 2 3 4 5
Comments

Key Result Area
Performance Expectations
Performance Evaluation
Rating 1 2 3 4 5
Comments

Key Result Area
Performance Expectations
Performance Evaluation
Rating 1 2 3 4 5
Comments

Additional Comments

Employee Comments

Employee Signature   Appraiser Signature

CHAPTER 6

LEADERSHIP AND TEAM-BUILDING

Influencing Employees to Work Effectively and Achieve Corporate Goals

"The task of the leader is to get his people from where they are to where they have not been."

—*Henry Kissinger*

I t is often said employees don't leave the organization, they leave the manager. While it is invariably true that good leaders are crucial to staff retention, they are also much more. Good leaders are the fundamental ingredient to sustained organizational success. A number of factors affect staff retention. Organizations that hold onto employees create a work environment that is attractive to the people who are critical to organizational success. These companies don't think of employees as workers but treat them as associates or partners.

Among the many factors that affect staff retention, the most

Great leadership creates a supportive work environment, challenging work, recognition and respect.

fundamental component is the presence of people-centered leadership. The quality of leadership, especially in supervisory roles, impacts the quality of work life and improves the organization's ability to retain employees. It is great leadership that creates a supportive work environment, challenging work, recognition and respect. When leaders focus on people, the organization will also typically have competitive compensation and benefits programs. But quality leadership means much more than simply ensuring low staff turnover.

The most successful leaders do not fit the popular media image of an ultra charismatic, larger-than-life character. Rather, organizations need leaders that can staff the organization with the right people, recognize the challenges and opportunities facing the organization, establish and implement an appropriate strategic direction, and drive the organization to continually innovate and succeed. Success depends on the ability to implement the strategic plan and adapt when circumstances require changes. Great leaders combine excellence in people management and strategic implementation. They create an environment that makes people want to stick around.

LEADERSHIP

A leader is a person you will follow to a place you wouldn't go by yourself, a manager tells you where to go.

The qualities of a good leader have been studied and postulated to death and the list of attributes is very long. Regardless of their position or claim to leadership, there are a few key traits that true leaders demonstrate; these are traits they cultivate and demonstrate as a matter of choice, not title or job role. Leaders who are effective in the "little ways" strive for the following in their interactions and their work:

The manager administers.	*The leader innovates.*
The manager has a short-range view.	*The leader has a long-range perspective.*
The manager asks how and when.	*The leader asks what and why.*
The manager has his eye on the bottom line.	*The leader has his eye on the horizon.*
The manager accepts the status quo.	*The leader challenges it.*

They're Present

Leaders pay attention to what they're doing at the moment or to whom they're speaking at the moment. Unlike those folks who are clearly "somewhere else" when you're talking with them, you don't feel unseen, unrecognized or unheard in a leader's presence.

They Listen

Because they're present and paying attention, leaders don't just remember talking with you, they remember what you said. After talking with leader's, you don't think to yourself, "Gee, I may have just as well spoken to the wall."

They Speak Mindfully

Leaders are conscious that their words have an effect on others, so they speak consciously. Unlike the stories of the unfortunate buffoons who scream and yell at executive meetings making people cower, leaders don't need to rely on such antics.

They Encourage

Leaders, being grounded and secure in themselves, find it easier to be encouraging of others. They encourage others to take risks, to pick themselves up after making mistakes, to take their skills to the next level, to pursue their dreams.

Great leaders listen, support and encourage.

Welcome
Changes
We all can
make a difference
& together we
will make a
better Salon

By
218

we want to improve the
quality of our
sales people thru feedback Education
& coaching — results in
a greater quantity of sales

(our goal service reps
requesting
Your job is a one of Sales.
& we all need to work
together to achieve

Performance Planning
" Focusing
" Assessment
Your expectation for Success

Confront and
diagnose problems
&, jointly
develop
solutions
Discuss
performances
& document

Post on R.C.S.D.
& J Wales Web
Site - Job opportunities

0412-71441

Gave me
an example
of self motivation

specify
probation
period Pg 136

Pg 46

for Job

Gave examples
of multi-tasking
gave aid on game
various job in
unrelated areas

BOB'S BUCKS

BIRTHDAY
calender

Assumption

Template

could Interview ?
have applicant Pg 69, 70, 71, 73 ?
imagine

69, 70, 71, 73 ?
82, 132, 149, 152
217, 323
BOB 227
238, 233 smart
233, 239,

3 to be
printed
v for following orders
Time to respond

Bottom 87, 88, 110

applicant agrees to work flexible
hours which include: but not
limited to Sat & Sun. and
beyond posted evening hours
to service customers

Pg 230. Reviews
are open &
honest & provide
positive & negative
feedback

They're Honest

Real leaders strive to know themselves so that they have the inner resources to speak, live and lead honestly. Leaders don't say one thing in public while doing something else more self-serving in private. Leaders don't have to make excuses about poor behavior; if it's unethical, they'll find another way to do it.

They're Humble

Real leaders know the long-term costs of arrogance are high. Great leaders have always shown great humility, which allows them to cultivate the leadership traits that truly serve themselves and others.

They Persevere

Leaders know that failures and difficulties are not ends, but simply doors to pass through on the way to greater wisdom and skillfulness.

They're Courageous

Leaders know that everyone, themselves included, feels fearful at times. Leaders don't, however, let their fears and uncertainties stop them from persevering, from pursuing their dreams, from building their skillfulness or from speaking honestly.

They're Thoughtful

Leaders have the presence of mind to recognize others, whether when saying hello during the day, or paying a compliment for work well-done. Being thoughtful of others, leaders are on time for meetings, are conscious of using time well, are organized, follow through on promises and close the loop on communications.

They're Respectful

Leaders treat others respectfully and require that others are respectful in return. True leaders do not tolerate being spoken to or otherwise treated in a disrespectful manner, and, quite frankly, it is a rare occurrence for that to happen.

WHAT TYPE OF LEADER ARE YOU?

There are a variety of methods to discover what type of leader you are and a variety of names given to the various leadership types. Some models are based on personality traits, others are based on conflict resolution style, and others consider your behavioral style. The different types of leaders are endless: leaders can be classified as supportive, directive, authentic, empathic, transformational, motivational, laissez-faire, autocratic, consultative, participative, or a whole host of other categories depending on the evaluation tool used. While the actual name of the leadership style you employ may be many different things, essentially you determine the direction alone or you let others participate in determining the direction. There are as many different theories about which type of leadership is the best or most effective as there are names for different leadership styles. What seems to be important to all of the discussions on leadership is the need to be flexible and adaptive when applying a leadership style to a certain situation or a certain individual.

Adaptive Leadership

Situational (adaptive) leadership was developed by Paul Hersey and Ken Blanchard, and is based on the amount of direction and support a leader must provide given the situation and level of development of the employee in relation to the task. Development of the employee is based on his or her commitment level and competence. The four different types of leadership are: Directing, Influencing, Collaborating, and Delegating. Each situation requires awareness of the type of support and direction needed and then the appropriate leadership style is applied.

Directing

Leader behavior is directive and is used when an employee is not ready to perform a task or set of tasks. The leader controls the process, teaches the basics, and used a directive style.

Influencing

Leader behavior is influential. While still closely managing the work that needs to be done, the leader coaches by counseling, mentoring and tutoring the employee; inspiring and acknowledging the success the person is achieving.

Collaborating

Leader behavior is consultative. The leader involves the employee in decision-making, invites ideas or draws them out and focuses discussions. It is a team-oriented approach.

Delegating

Leader behavior is trusting. The leader can let go, authorize and determine "what" rather than "how" work gets done. Trust is also the highest form of motivation.

WORKPLACE ISSUES AND LEADERSHIP EXAMPLES	
Situation	**Leadership Strategy:** Delegating
An employee has been with the company for three years and has mastered her work so well that she can teach it to new hires. Her motivation is slumping because she has little more to learn. What leadership approach best suits her situation?	This employee can and should be trusted to direct her own work. The leader is responsible for determining what needs to get done, and the rest is up to her. Because she knows the job so well, given a little trust and encouragement, she will probably come up with innovative (and cost-saving!) ways to get the job done and contribute more effectively to the company.
Situation	**Leadership Strategy:** Influencing
An employee, laid off from another organization was hired five months ago. His skill level is high, but he still hasn't grasped the company's ways of doing things. How do you lead him?	This employee does not need constant direction; what he needs is support to give him confidence in working within the policies and procedures of his new company. His leader needs to act as a mentor and coach; showing him the ropes and then letting him know when he is doing well or helping him to learn from his mistakes. With just enough support, this employee will become comfortable in his position and confident in his abilities.

Situation	Leadership Strategy: Directing
One of the most competent and dedicated employees asks for a transfer to a different job within the company in order to increase his versatility. From welding he goes to receiving. What style of management is appropriate for this person?	This employee is not ready to do the actual tasks of a receiver. In order for him not to get discouraged, he will need to be directed in his daily tasks until he has mastered them. Because his competence was so high in the welding department, if he is not given enough support and direction to learn his new job, he will come to see himself as a failure and his self-esteem, motivation and commitment will plummet.
Situation	**Leadership Strategy:** Collaborating:
An employee has been with the company for two years and does a modestly competent job in most tasks. She is not a star but a very dependable and capable worker. What style do you use I this situation?	While many mangers would be tempted to use an influencing style with this employee, she will not grow and realize her potential unless her manager collaborates with her. This participation will give her the confidence she needs to break out of the average rut and really earn praise and recognition. By including her in discussions and getting her input, the manager is saying that this employee is valued.

With a growing emphasis on tasks and results, supervisors have become less concerned with employee development. Unfortunately, this hard-pressure, results-oriented relationship between the supervisor and the employee tends to generate increasing levels of underperformance in the workplace. When employees are labeled underperformers, what really occurs in many cases is a mismatch between the manager's style of supervision and the employee's level of dependence or independence. What managers have to understand is that each employee relates to authority differently. Some workers need close supervision while others thrive when working on their own. Many people make the transition from dependence on authority to self-reliance without help, but still others are stuck at specific stages and need some catalyst to move to the next level of independent performance.

Managers need to understand is that each employee relates to authority differently.

The reality is that each employee can be effectively stimulated to perform better simply through the impact of the supervisor's leadership.

LEADERSHIP PROBLEMS AND SOLUTIONS EXAMPLE 1	
Situation	**Problem**
An employee with limited skills was assigned the front desk reception function at a small company. The individual quickly earned the label of a "non-performer" because she did not find work on her own. Many assignments were not completed and those that were seemed to take forever, with results below expectations. She did manage the telephone reception really well, but that requirement was a limited portion of her job. The only training she received was based on self-help modules that she had to learn on her own.	It turns out that the supervisor was not providing this particular employee enough support.
Solution	
The supervisor was given instructions on how to direct work during an assignment, help the individual decide what to do and how to do it, and review each assignment for effectiveness and improvement needed. With support, the non-performing employee began to understand what makes each assignment work well. Her assignments were increasingly successful, earning her recognition from each of the people assigning her. Today, this employee initiates, creates and completes work at a level that impresses her supervisors.	

LEADERSHIP PROBLEMS AND SOLUTIONS EXAMPLE 2

Situation	Problem
An individual, who without much formal training, had learned to be a computer programmer. This employee was instructed and directed by a senior programmer who literally solved all problems. Recently, a change in the employee's behavior was observed. The individual began to complete work in his own time frame. He also began to show resentment toward the constant instruction from the supervising programmer. The greater the pressure from the supervisor, the more the employee backed away and seemed to work less. On the other hand, he was indicating that there were projects that he wanted to add to his workload, which always seemed to be in conflict with the supervisor's priorities.	This individual was outgrowing his supervisor's style of work. He wanted to become less dependent and take more initiative, but had not developed enough confidence to take on projects that were important enough to put him at risk and challenge his skills. At the same time, he was irritated by the constant overseeing of his work by his supervisor. The supervisor, focused as he was on tasks and results, had no awareness of his employee's growth and development and continued to insist that the individual conform to his style of direct supervision. It was later found that the employee was taking his work home to escape the constant overview. He was also becoming angry that he could not break from the patterns that were the preferred style of his supervisor.

Solution

The supervisor learned how to back away and supervise from a critical results path (Collaborating) instead of detailed analysis (Directing) of the employee's work. At the same time, the two had to learn how to inject creativity into the employee's projects.

So-called underperformance occurs at every level within a company, even in the most senior leadership roles. These blocks to performance are very often caused by a mismatch between the supervisor's expectations and the employee's stage of development. While there is a complex interaction between employees and supervisors, understanding the critical transition that occurs for every employee, within a wide range of circumstances, will better enable supervisors to draw out better levels of performance. The key factor is how authority and the employee's reaction to it can best be managed to help the employee develop independence. Improved performance results when managers learn this single most important supervisory skill, which is adaptive leadership.

AUTHENTICITY—THE NEW LEADERSHIP BUZZ WORD

Webster defines authentic as "worthy of acceptance or belief, conforming to fact or reality, trustworthy, not imaginary, false or imitation." Our sense of people's authenticity has an enormous impact on how much we trust them, how comfortable we are with them and how willing we are to follow them. It is clear, then, why authenticity is so important to be an effective leader.

What are the consequences when a leader is perceived as not being authentic? There is a significant impact on trust. People are less likely to volunteer ideas or information the leader needs to know. They are more likely to question the motives of the leader. They are less likely to give that leader their all. These undercurrents sap the energy of any team or organization, and trust and camaraderie are lost in this type of work environment.

What causes leaders to be inauthentic? Some people come across as guarded or secretive because they are naturally cautious or reserved. This tends to make people uncomfortable when that person is the formal leader because they wonder what he or she is thinking or feeling. Individuals in leadership positions who have this kind of personality do well to consider ways to reduce this uneasiness in others. Finding ways to communicate that are comfortable for all involved

Some people come across as guarded or secretive because they are naturally cautious or reserved.

makes a significant positive impact as can increasing the amount of communication if it has previously been sparse.

Cultural conditioning from our old hierarchical models can cause some leaders, especially those in formal management positions, to believe that to be genuine and vulnerable is a sign of weakness. Coupled with that is a belief that they must know, or at least look like they know, all the answers. But this is not the source of power of really effective leaders. Ultimately, leadership is more about who you are than what you know.

Thoughts on Authenticity and Leadership

"Authenticity means not being plastic, not being some artificial creation. I think authenticity is a vital, essential piece of integrity and that goes back to trust and respect. I don't think leaders can be effective leaders if they are not authentic. If people detect that you are not who you say you are, then you're dead."

—L. B. "Bud" Mingledorff, President, Mingledorff's Inc., Norcross

"I think authenticity is part of integrity. Being genuine, not manipulating, being true to yourself and your beliefs, not putting up a façade and not being unreachable. When leaders are not authentic and try to create an image, I think people are too smart for that and they see straight through it. Everybody is vulnerable. Nobody is Superman. Hopefully, we are not putting in place as leaders people who think they are supermen. I think, too, that the more self-confidence you have, the easier it is to be vulnerable. Being self-confident also means that people can critique you and you will not be defensive and you will take it very constructively the way it's meant to be. Then you can know that it's maybe not who you are, but what you are doing, and what you are doing you can change. I also think that it's extremely important that leaders share with their people how they feel and what they think. You can share feelings without getting too personal."

—Ulf Petersson, President, Megadoor, Inc., Peachtree City

"Authenticity works hand in hand with passion because you can't manifest passion without authenticity. It just won't fly. I also think that leaders are respected in part because they are genuine, au-

thentic and want to share something positive with you and help you in some way."

—Dave Schmit, Senior Vice President, Morrison Homes

To grow as leaders, we must be constantly growing ourselves. Some questions to ask yourself as you grow your leadership abilities:

- What are my beliefs about what it takes to be a good leader?

- What are my beliefs and expectations about myself as a leader?

- Am I willing and able to be open, authentic and vulnerable?

- Do I have healthy self-esteem and self-confidence that allow me to be genuinely open to feedback and to the risk of making mistakes?

- Do my communication style and frequency clearly and honestly convey my views as leader?

Tips for Leadership Success

- Assume responsibility for your own actions. If you are not successful, don't blame anyone else. Take it on the chin and learn from it.

- Assume responsibility for your emotional reactions. It's not what happens to you that matters; it's what it means to you that determines your reaction. Stand back and get perspective. Ask yourself, "What can we learn from this?"; it's easier to control yourself.

- Identify the potential in each of your subordinates. Remember that people tend to live up to our expectations of them. Let your people know how terrific you think they are.

- Make an inventory of the resources at your disposal and use those resources to help your staff perform better. We live in a world of limited resources. Given that restraint, how can you optimize the results your department delivers?

- Be optimistic. Optimism is contagious; so is pessimism. If your team is going to develop a positive, can-do attitude, you will need to set the tone.

- Develop a team vision for your department. Define what the team will become—make it inspiring! This is particularly powerful when you develop your vision as a team.

- Set specific and measurable goals to make that vision come true. Include time frames and resource requirements.

- Treat others with empathy and respect—no matter what. Gain the independence, power and self-respect that come from doing the right thing, without regard to what others do.

- Think less about your own needs and more about the needs of your team. You will reap what you sow.

- Set an example — be a high performer. Work hard and smart. People will follow your example. Be honest with yourself and your team. Realize that, eventually, people who work with you will know you for who you are. Be open to their criticism and learn from it.

- Set a schedule for your own training and development — stick to it. Keep yourself growing and motivated. You're worth it.

- Model your leadership style after someone who inspires you. It's hard work to cut a path through the woods; it's much simpler to walk in someone else's tracks.

- Good input = good output. Find and consistently use good sources of management guidance for reading, viewing and listening.

TEAMWORK

Teamwork is the fuel that allows common people to attain uncommon results.

What is a good leader without a team to lead? The reason we want to develop leadership qualities is to build a strong team that will accomplish more than our best individual effort. Teamwork has become an essential element of almost every job in today's labor market, and it is very important for business leaders to know how to develop and maintain a strong team culture.

A Teamwork Metaphor

Canadian geese always fly in a V formation. The reason for this pattern is that the flapping wings in front create an updraft for the geese in the back. Studies have shown that this V formation results in a 71 percent increase in the range of flight compared to that of a single goose. On long flights, individual geese take turns leading the flock; when the lead goose gets tired, it slips back in the formation where the flying is easier and lets a well-rested goose take over the strenuous lead position. If a goose strays away from the flock, it returns quite quickly because it can't hope to keep up without the support of the geese's flapping wings. The geese in the rear of the V formation honk loudly, encouraging and supporting the leader. The leader doesn't honk—he preserves his energy for flying. If a goose is injured or somehow falls out of formation, two other geese accompany it to the ground where they nurture and attend to their companion until it is either able to return to the flock or dies.

This example of working together highlights many of the important attributes of effective teams and teamwork.

Principles of Effective Teams

- Effective teams have independent members. The productivity and efficiency of the unit is determined by the coordinated, interactive efforts of all its members.

- Effective teams help members be more efficient working together than alone. An effective team outperforms even the best individual's best effort.

- Effective teams function so well that they create their own magnetism. Team members desire to affiliate with a team because of the advantages of membership.

- Effective teams do not always have the same leader. Leadership responsibility is rotated among the highly skilled team members.

- Effective teams have members who care for and nurture one another. No team member is undervalued or under appreciated; all are treated as integral to the team's success.

- Effective teams have members who cheer loudly for the leader. Mutual encouragement is given and received freely.

- Effective teams have a high level of trust among members. Members are as much interested in others' success as their own.

WHAT IS A TEAM?

It is important to remember that a team is not just a group of people stuck together working on a project or task. A team is a group of people working together to achieve something bigger and better than any of the individual team members could accomplish or even think possible.

Groups vs. Teams	
Groups *A set of individuals who rely on the sum of "individual bests" for their performance.*	**Teams** *A small number of people with complementary skills who are committed to a common purpose, common performance goals and a common approach for which they hold themselves mutually accountable.*
Little communication	Plenty of opportunity for discussion
No support	Plenty of support
Lack of vision	Process of discovery supported by openness and honesty
Exclusive cliques	Tactical and work groups combine easily into a single team
The whole is less than the sum of its parts	The whole is greater than the sum of its parts
Seeks to hide its identity	Seeks to discover its identity
Leaves new members to find their own way but insists on conformity	Welcomes new members by showing them existing norms and openness to change
Leader manipulates the team to own ends	Leader seeks team decisions by serving the team as a focus for two-way communication

TEAM-BUILDING

A team is not built overnight—it takes a great deal of concerted effort to transform a scraggly group of individuals into a true team. There are essentially four stages of team building and each has its own challenges which all demand different leadership skills. To build and lead an effective team, it is important to understand these stages and adapt your style to help the team through the transitions. Effective leadership requires helping the team through the early stages of development, where a team is struggling to become a coherent entity, to a more mature stage of development, when the team has become a highly effective, smoothly functioning organization. The four stages are as follows:

There are four steps to building an effective team.

Stage 1: Awareness (Forming)

This is the stage when a group of people gets together and realizes that they have a common purpose. They make a commitment to achieve a certain outcome, and each team member accepts their responsibility in the process. In the initial stages of team development, the leader has to bring other members up to speed on the mission. The leader's job is to create cohesion amongst these individuals chosen for a team and the team members are likely uncertain about their role in the whole process. Very seldom do new team members want to question the leader for fear of appearing "out of the loop," and, likewise, they don't want to answer the leader's questions in case the answer is wrong.

At the beginning, it's all about self-protection, so the team leader has to deal head-on with the challenge, and that means taking charge and directing the process. There is plenty of opportunity for free and open discussion once the team is formed and comfortable, but now you must focus on direction, clarity and structure.

This is why many teams fail to ever become effective: they get stuck in the forming stage and never really become a team; they remain a group in team clothing. This doesn't mean you can rush the forming stage. It is imperative that the team members have time to explore and clarify the guidelines, boundaries and expectations and reveal their uncertainties. When the team leader successfully provides the necessary clarity and structure, the team can move on to the second stage.

Attributes of Team Development While Forming

Team Member Questions	Interpersonal Relationships	Task Issues	Effective Leader Behavior
Who are these other people?	Silence	Orient members	Make introductions
What is going to happen?	Self-consciousness	Become comfortable with team membership	Answer questions
What is expected of me?	Dependence	Establish trust	Establish a foundation of trust
Where are we headed and why?	Superficiality	Establish relationship with leaders	Model expected behaviors
What are our goals?	Reactivity	Establish clarity of purpose	Clarify goals, procedures, rules, expectations
How do I fit in?	Uncertainty	Deal with feelings of independence	Foster team spirit

Stage 2: Conflict (Storming)

At this stage, the team is formed and now the members feel comfortable with one another: maybe too comfortable, because this is when the conflict surfaces. The team is suddenly dealing with issues of power, leadership and decision-making. Team members are no longer uncertain of their roles and they all have committed to achieving the team's goals and contributing to its success. This naturally means that individual team members will disagree on methods, actions, decisions and opinions. Individual differences have been suppressed for the sake of the team, but this "honeymoon" stage does not last forever. The leader's role in all of this is to diffuse the conflict while validating all the arguments and mediating solutions.

The storming stage does not mean that the team disintegrates into chaos and turmoil; it just means that effective ways to deal with conflict have to be developed and agreed upon. The team leader is responsible for spearheading this conflict resolution "charter" and fostering a win-win result. Throughout this process, it is important to let your team know that this type of conflict is normal and it is not a sign of dysfunction. Many people have been socialized to avoid conflict so it may be necessary to overtly let the team know that it is okay to voice their opinions and that the divergent thinking within a team is exactly what spurns teams on to greater efficiency than any one individual effort.

The leader has an especially crucial role during the storming stage. The vision or goal that brought the team together in the first place must be emphasized and reinforced. The danger to avoid, though, is the phenomenon of "groupthink" where preserving the team takes precedence over sound decision-making and suddenly there is very little conflict. The storming stage is a good time to shake things up a bit, let other members lead certain projects and encourage team members to cross-train and teach others. Emphasize the interdependence of the team members and reward the team for its accomplishments. This builds commitment and unity and prepares the team to get busy and get to work.

Attributes of Team Development While Storming

Team Member Questions	Interpersonal Relationships	Task Issues	Effective Leader Behavior
How will we handle disagreements?	Polarization of team members	Manage conflict	Identify a common enemy and reinforce the vision
How will we communicate negative information?	Coalitions or cliques form	Legitimize productive expression of individuality	Generate a commitment among team members
Can the team be changed?	Competition	Overcome "groupthink"	Turn students into teachers
How can we make decisions amidst disagreement?	Disagreement with the leader	Examine key work processes of the team	Be an effective mediator
Do we really need this leader?	Challenging others' viewpoints	Turn counter dependence into inter-dependence	Provide individual and team recognition
Do I want to stay a part of the team?	Expressing individuality		Foster win-win thinking

Stage 3:   Cooperation (Norming)

Once teams emerge from the storming stage, they are very confident they can handle anything that is thrown at them. The norming stage of team development is characterized by cohesiveness as team members discover that they in fact do have common interests with each other. They learn to appreciate their differences, they work better together and they problem-solve together. Norming is also a time to sit back and assess just how much the team has accomplished. Feedback is especially important at this stage, and the team should experience some successes to reinforce their commitment.

Norming can be a time of complacence, though, so the leader must continue to generate enthusiasm and spark team members' interest. The team is starting to look like a well-oiled machine and this is not the time to relax and ease up on proactive leadership. The way that teams continue to be successful is through constant effort and attention so you will always need to keep the fire lit. Be supportive and complimentary, use humor and playfulness and build strong coalitions within the team. These

Norming can be a time of complacence, so the leader must continue to generate enthusiasm and spark team members' interest.

behaviors will confirm your involvement and commitment to the team as well as provide affirmation that the team is doing a good job.

Attributes of Team Development While Norming

Team Member Questions	Interpersonal Relationships	Task Issues	Effective Leader Behavior
Will we be able to stay together?	Cooper-ativeness	Maintain unity and cohesiont	Ensures the team experiences some success
How can we be successful as a team?	Commitment to a team vision	Differentiate and clarify roles	Facilitate role differentiation
What is my relationship to the team leader and other team members?	Inter-dependence	Determine levels of personal investment	Show support to team members
What role do I play?	Supportive	Clarify the future	Provide feedback
How do we measure up to other teams?	Complacence	Decide on a level of commitment to the team's future	Articulate a vision for the team
Can we take this all the way?	Self-doubt	Deal with feelings of independence	Generate commitment to the vision

Stage 4:   Productivity (Performing)

This is the stage when the team synergy really takes off and it becomes apparent that it is capable of setting and accomplishing really innovative and progressive goals. The team is functioning as a highly effective and efficient unit because it has worked through all the issues embedded in the previous stages and can now focus on performance. The team members themselves also change their focus and look for ways to improve processes and find innovative solutions. Each team member is confident of the role they play and they are self-sufficient, but their connection to the other team members ensures they are committed to learning, developing and improving.

The team leader is now a delegator. In that role, you have to listen to your team members and bring their ideas forward for the team to evaluate. It is important to support the team in their decisions and provide the resources necessary for success. The team leader is not the source of all the good ideas, and by enabling other team members' ideas, the whole team becomes more effective. Team leaders see to it that the activities are coordinated and that innovative suggestions are introduced and fit into the team's plans, but the team is now effectively self-managed and very competent. It is akin to a parent sending their child off to college; they will always be there for support and guidance, but they trust that they have given their child the tools he or she needs to go out and be successful.

Attributes of Team Development While Performing

Team Member Questions	Interpersonal Relationships	Task Issues	Effective Leader Behavior
How can we continuously improve?	High mutual trust	Capitalize on core competence	Foster innovative and continuous improvement at the same time
How can we foster creativity?	Unconditional team commitment	Foster continuous improvement	Advance the quality culture of the team
How can we build on our core competence?	Multifaceted relationships among team members	Anticipate needs of customers and respond in advance of requests	Provide regular, ongoing feedback on team performance
What improvements can be made to our processes?	Mutual training and development	Enhance speed and timeliness	Champion team members ideas and provide additional resources
How can we maintain this high energy level?	Entrepreneur-ship	Encourage creative problem-solving	Help to avoid slipping back to previous stages

TEAM-BUILDING IS:	TEAM-BUILDING IS NOT:
• A way of life.	• A short term, flavor of the month.
• The responsibility of every team member.	• Imposed without regard to peoples' feelings.
• A continuous process.	• Spasmodic.
• About developing a clear and unique identity.	• Reserved for only some members of the team.
• Focused on a clear and consistent set of goals.	• An excuse for not meeting personal responsibilities.
• Concerned with the needs and ambitions of each team member recognizing the unique contribution that each individual can make.	• A process where actions clearly contradict intentions.
• An awareness of the potential of the team as a unit.	• Seen as a chore.
• Results oriented.	
• Enjoyable.	

AN EFFECTIVE TEAM

An effective team is one that has worked through the various stages of team-building and emerged intact. Teams go through phases and even though the goal is to get to and remain in the performing stage, there are setbacks that occur. New direction, new team members, new leadership: these can all cause confusion within the team and threaten its stability, but if team members stay committed to the core characteristics of effective teams, then they should be able to withstand the pressures.

Successful, effective teams demonstrate high achievement in the following areas:

Appropriate Leadership
The leader has all the skills and desire to develop and use a team approach and is prepared to allocate time for team-building activities. He or she acts as a facilitator on the team. An inappropriate leader is unwilling or unable to develop a team approach and does not encourage team-building activities. He or she does not share power or leadership responsibilities

Suitable Membership
Members are individually qualified and bring a mix of skills, experiences and perspectives that provide a balanced group. An unsuitable member is not socially or professional qualified to contribute to the team and, thus, does not help it to achieve its goals.

Commitment to the Team's Success
Members are committed to the goals of the team and achieving them. They are willing to devote personal time to developing the team and supporting their fellow team members.

Positive Climate
People are relaxed, open, direct and prepared to take risks.

Achievement Focus
Team goals are clear, considered worthwhile, require some "stretching," but are achievable. Performance is frequently reviewed to find ways to improve.

Relevant Corporate Role

The significance of the distinctive ways in which the team contributes to the corporate goals and strategies are clear and understood. In effective teams, the team is excluded from corporate planning and is not given or does not understand the "big picture."

Effective Work Methods

There are systematic problem-solving methods, structured decision-making techniques and skills for conducting productive meetings.

Role Clarity

Team roles are clearly defined and communication patterns are developed. Administrative procedures are in place that supports a team approach.

Constructive Criticism

Feedback about team and individual errors and weaknesses are constructively and positively provided and used as a learning experience. Ineffective teams use soft critiquing: In order not to upset any team members, neither team nor individual errors are addressed directly and thoroughly enough to eliminate them.

Individual Development

The positive team climate and support helps members to achieve their personal potential. Ineffective teams have members who have not developed the maturity and confidence needed to be assertive or deal with other members' strong personalities.

Creative Strength

The team encourages and generates new ideas from the interaction of members, rewards risk-taking, and puts good ideas into action.

Positive Inter-Group Relations

Members are encouraged to work with others for the common good. Relationships with other teams are systematically developed to identify opportunities for collaboration. Negative inter-group relations are characterized by competition and conflicting priorities.

An effective team is a high-performing unit whose members are actively interdependent and committed to working together for a common purpose. A team is a performance unit and the "acid test" is its ability to consistently achieve desired results. To do so, members of successful teams are committed to continuous quality improvement. They regularly review their experiences, assess the strengths and weaknesses of their process and constructively criticize both individual and team performance. When team members identify blockages to effectiveness, they work together to clear the way for further success through team-development.

The theory of teams is great and we can all see how the team concept works. But, as much as we are committed to build a strong team, there are one or two employees who make the process difficult. Despite our best efforts, and after reading every interpersonal relationship book ever written, there are still some participants who are disruptive and difficult. This is a huge challenge for team leaders, and the way these difficult members are handled sets the tone and culture of the team. Does the team become intolerant and exclusionary, or does it seek to support and collaborate with all of its members using every available open communication and conflict-resolution technique known to man? Here are some suggestions for handling some of the typical examples of difficult team members.

HANDLING DIFFICULT TEAM MEMBERS		
Type	**Behavior or Comments**	**Suggested Response**
Hostile	"It'll never work." "That's a typical touchy, feely response."	"How do others here feel about this?" "It seems we have a different perspective on the details, but do we agree on the principles?"
Know-it-all	"I have an MBA from Harvard and…" "Let me tell ya, in my 30 years at this company…"	"Let's review the facts…" "Another noted authority has said…"
Loud-mouth	Constantly blurts out ideas and tries to dominate meetings and discussions.	Interrupt and ask, "Can you summarize your main point?" "I appreciate your comments, but we should also hear from Susan…"
Interrupter	Starts talking before others are finished.	"Wait a minute Carol, let's here what Stu was saying."

Interpreter	"What he's really trying to say is…" "Yeah, Mike's got a point. He's telling us that…"	"Let's let Mike speak for himself." "Mike, did Roy correctly understand what you were saying?"
Gossiper	"I heard the CFO say that…" "There's a new policy coming out that says…"	"Until we verify what was said, let's continue as planned." "Has anyone else heard about this new development?"
Silent Distracter	Reads, rolls eyes, shakes their head, crosses arms, etc.	Direct questions to them to determine their level of expertise and interest. Draw them into the discussion and try to build an alliance.

An Effective Team Leader:

- Communicates.

- Is open, honest and fair.

- Uses participative decision-making.

- Acts consistently.

- Gives all team members information necessary to do their job.

- Sets goals and emphasizes them.

- Keeps focused and follows-up regularly.

- Listens to feedback without defensiveness and ask questions.

- Shows loyalty.

- Creates an atmosphere of growth.

- Has wide visibility.

- Gives praise and recognition.

- Criticizes constructively and addresses problems directly.

- Develops plans.

- Displays tolerance and flexibility.

- Demonstrates assertiveness.

- Treats all members with respect.

- Accepts ownership for team decisions.

- Represents the team and stands up for its decisions and actions.

- Creates energy and excitement.

- Stimulates creativity in others.

- Acts as a sounding board, helping people think through their issues.

- Enforces standards (deals gently, promptly, but firmly with noncompliance).

Teams are everywhere, and it is critical for business leaders, managers and supervisors to learn how to function effectively within a team environment. This means fostering a team culture, building a strong team and keeping the team operational and optimized. Not all groups are teams, and using the word "team" in your organization does not necessarily mean your employees are actually functioning as one. Look at the effectiveness of your workplace and that will be your first clue as to whether you have a team environment. Effective teams are highly productive so it is worth the time investigating and working toward your own team culture.

CHAPTER 7

EMPLOYEE RETENTION ESSENTIALS
Influencing Employees to Work Effectively

"Build it and they will stay."

—*Anonymous*

A positive work attitude creates a corporate culture that attracts and retains the most talented employees. By creating a team spirit, you will keep your good employees. When people are part of a group that is making a difference and enjoying their work, they will build loyalty and trust; those two characteristics will ensure your employees stay with you. Keep them aware of their role and accountable for their success and their commitment will follow.

It sounds difficult, and no doubt does require a concerted effort, but it can be done and needs to be done if you intend to manage your human resources as strategically as your financial and material ones. Businesspeople everywhere espouse that without their employees there would be no company, but few actually put that ideal into practice. It starts with a solid foundation of employee recruitment and hiring and is built on by effective communication, motivation, training and leadership. Above all, it is trusting yourself and your company leaders to manage with their heart—apply the golden rule and "do unto others as you would have others do unto you."

Effective people-management is really about treating people with the respect and dignity they deserve. It is not about developing policies that address every little nuance that has happened or might happen in the workplace; it's about using your brain, your heart and your gut, and then doing what needs to be done while preserving your employees' dignity and self-esteem. The flip side of that is doing whatever is appropriate to develop and enhance your employees' dignity and self-esteem.

Effective people-management is really about treating people with the respect and dignity they deserve.

The reasons people leave organizations are not complicated. Nor are solutions to address fundamental issues which influence how an individual feels about themselves and their work.

REFRAME THE CHALLENGE

Instead of asking "What do I need to do to keep you?" ask "What do I need to do to ensure you are happy and engaged by your work?"

Think like a marketer by appealing to the heart as well as the mind and the pocketbook. The new worker is loyal to his or her work and the people he or she works with or for. Excite people through the challenges of the work, not by the company they work for.

Promote Career Self-Assessment

One common reason people leave jobs is that they imagine that other people in other jobs are getting tons of stock options and bonuses, more love and appreciation for their work and maybe even time for a life. At the same time, they underestimate how their job is in fact a better match than they think

Most people who go through a career assessment are surprised to discover they are actually much happier than they thought.

it is. Most people who go through a career assessment are surprised to discover they are actually much happier than they thought.

Often, one or two things have had a disproportionate impact in coloring how they feel — they have generalized from the specific "I want more team work." to "I can't stand this job." Managers need to ask staff what it is that is most important to them and how can they support them in getting what they want.

Know What You Cannot Change

Some of these needs can be addressed and some cannot. For example, there will always be people who are unhappy because of a fundamental mismatch between their needs and the mission of the organization. A person who has decided to change in mid-career from the for-profit sector who is looking to give something back to society, or someone who can't take even the most benign office politics, is going to leave no matter what you do. These are not problems an organization or manager can address in a meaningful way. These are issues that need to be identified and fully explored at the recruitment and hiring stage. Remember, employee fit is just as important, if not more important, than skills, abilities and qualifications.

Improve Work-Life Balance

Work-life balance is an issue with which everyone is struggling, and is probably the most significant bargaining chip an employer has. The new worker aggressively evaluates the effort-reward equation. When people are working 100 hours a week, they are vulnerable to approaches from recruiters who promise either significantly more money or more discretionary control over their time. Sabbaticals, alternative work arrangements, telecommuting— everyone by now knows the drill about what today's harried worker needs, yet the report card on what organizations are actually doing is pitiful. Make your organization an employer of choice by actually offering these perks, and you'll be amazed at the return.

Work-life balance is an issue with which everyone is struggling.

Provide Skill-Building and Boredom-Fighting New Experiences

Feeling overworked and under-challenged is one of the most common forms of contemporary career stress. When people get bored, they will look for a new career opportunity. Although they are correct in their assessment that they are unhappy, the solution they come up with—a career move— may be overkill. People can be rejuvenated through a minor shift in work focus, a new set of collegial relationships or professional development. Smart managers will be creative in reshaping assignments to reengage staff intellectually.

Say Thank You and Mean It

Managers recognize contributions associated with each individual worker, but often they get so frenzied by their own demanding commitments that they fail to notice individual contributions. The best way to say thank you, and mean it, is with consistent performance appraisals and as much recognition as possible.

TRUTH IN HUMOR

Humor in the workplace can help lighten everyone's day. The following tongue-in-cheek "workplace tips" poke fun at some dubious management techniques.

10 Tips from Employees to Their Managers on How to Enhance the Relationship

Never give me work in the morning. Always wait until 5:00 and then bring it to me. The challenge of a deadline is refreshing.

If it's really a "rush job," run in and interrupt me every ten minutes to inquire how it's going. That helps.

Always leave without telling anyone where you're going. It gives me a chance to be creative when someone asks where you are.

If you give me more than one job to do, don't tell me which is the priority; let me guess.

Do your best to keep me late. I like the office and really have nowhere to go and nothing to do.

If a job I do pleases you, keep it a secret. Leaks like that could cost me a promotion.

7 If you don't like my work, tell everyone; I like my name to be popular in conversation.

8 If you have special instructions for a job, don't write them down. If fact, save them until the job is almost done.

9 Never introduce me to the people you're with. When you refer to them later, my shrewd deductions will identify them.

10 Be nice to me only when the job I'm doing for you could really change your life.

INDEX

Need a Quick Reference?

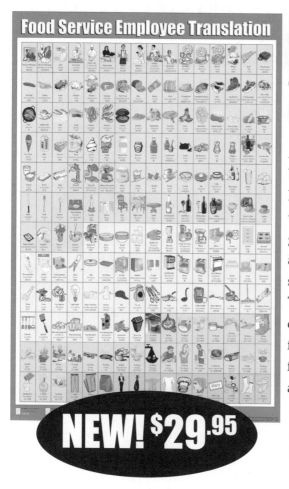

Improve Your Food Service Operation

From sales to service, the best food service reference books are here! Call **1-800-541-1336** and order today.

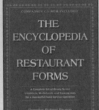

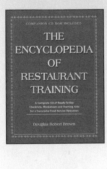

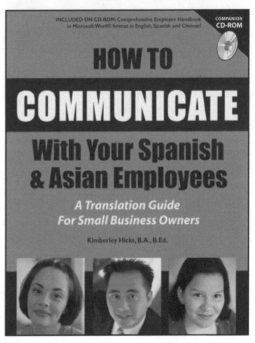